TALES FROM THE
MINNESOTA VIKINGS
SIDELINE

A COLLECTION OF THE GREATEST VIKINGS STORIES EVER TOLD

BY

BILL WILLIAMSON

WITH

ERIC THOMPSON

SPORTS
PUBLISHING

Sports Publishing books may be purchased in bulk at special discounts for sales promotion, corporate gifts, fund-raising, or educational purposes. Special editions can also be created to specifications. For details, contact the Special Sales Department, Sports Publishing, 307 West 36th Street, 11th Floor, New York, NY 10018 or sportspubbooks@skyhorsepublishing.com.

Sports Publishing® is a registered trademark of Skyhorse Publishing, Inc.®, a Delaware corporation.

Visit our website at www.sportspubbooks.com

10 9 8 7 6 5 4 3

Library of Congress Cataloging-in-Publication Data is available on file.
ISBN: 978-1-61321-224-0

Printed in the United States of America

Thank you, Coleen.

As with every accomplishment in my life, without my wife, Coleen Romero-Williamson, completing this book would have been impossible. Coleen spurs me to succeed—to be more than average.

The best part of her encouragement is that she doesn't realize she is doing so. I'm sure this dedication will embarrass her. She's not one for praise, or, as she says, "sappiness."

But it is her quiet encouragement that made taking on this project possible. Most of all, it is her unique support and understanding that has allowed me the time to attempt to be something special.

—Bill Williamson

I'd like to thank my incredible wife Carolyn for her unwavering support, encouragement, and ability to tolerate such an insanely intense football fan throughout the years.

—Eric Thompson

Acknowledgments

I'd like to thank all of the former and current Minnesota Vikings players, coaches, and support staff who took the time to share their memories and thoughts. It was quite a pleasure hearing them all.

I'd also like to thank my co-workers and supervisors at the *St. Paul Pioneer Press*, as well as my family and friends, for their support, knowledge, and encouragement.

–Bill Williamson

I'd like to thank Christopher Gates for starting an excellent Vikings blog, DailyNorseman.com, in 2006. Without the piece of internet real estate that he carved out back then, I would never have had the chance to cover the Vikings as I have and reach so many fellow fans today.

–Eric Thompson

Contents

Chapter 1

The Early Days

WHAT ELSE COULD IT BE?

The Minnesota franchise went about eight months without a nickname. After being awarded a franchise in January, 1960, the Twin Cities were thrilled about becoming a host to a NFL team, something that has had a profound effect on the community ever since.

But what would the franchise be named? Really, was there any other choice?

In one of his first moves with the team, new general manager Bert Rose quickly came up with the Vikings. After all, the name had great ties to the Nordic influence and flavor of the state. Plus, there aren't many tougher names.

So in one swift decision, the Vikings were born and horns started popping up throughout the state.

WHAT A START

The first few years of Vikings football were not spectacular, but one wouldn't know it by the first game in team history. The Vikings made the NFL take notice with a stunning victory over the well-established Chicago Bears at the Metrodome on Sept. 17, 1961.

The Vikings smoked the Bears 37-13, in what still stands as one of the biggest moments in team history.

Future legendary quarterback Fran Tarkenton, a third-round draft pick, came off the bench and sliced up the Bears, completing 17 of 23 pass attempts for 250 yards. He also threw four touchdown passes.

Fran Tarkenton: The scrambler made life tough for his offensive lineman, who had to keep up with him. The longer Tarkenton avoided pursuers, the more tired his protectors became.
(Photo by Rick A. Kolodziej)

AN UNRECOGNIZED DYNASTY

It bothers several former Vikings players and coaches that they're not included in the talks when it comes to the great teams of recent history, especially during the NFL's golden age of the 1970s.

The four-time Super Bowl-winning Pittsburgh Steelers are mentioned for their greatness, of course, but so are the Dallas Cowboys and Oakland Raiders, who also took home Lombardi Trophies during the decade. And then, of course, there are the great Miami Dolphins, who owned the early portion of the decade.

But what about the Vikings? They made four Super Bowl appearances between the 1969 and 1976 seasons. But perhaps because they lost all four Super Bowls, the Vikings aren't mentioned as one of the greats of the 1970s.

And it bothers them.

"We were great," running back Bill Brown said.

"We had everything. But I guess you have to win the Super Bowl for people to care."

The Vikings were star-studded on both sides of the ball. Their coach Bud Grant is considered one of the legends of the game, and future Hall of Famers Fran Tarkenton, Ron Yary, Alan Page and Paul Krause were all great leaders.

"It's still a mystery that we didn't win a Super Bowl," offensive line coach John Michels said. "We were a dynasty. For about four years there wasn't a better team in the NFL than us. But no one seems to remember it."

THE ONE THAT GOT AWAY

Some people have difficulty figuring which Vikings team was the best of the Bud Grant era.

Of course, there were four solid choices. They advanced to the Super Bowl after the 1969, 1973, 1974 and 1976 seasons. The core of the team was together for much of their Superbowl run.

But for running back Bill Brown—who was on the team for the first three Super Bowl appearances—it's really not much of a choice. It's the first of the Vikings' Super Bowl teams.

"The 1969 team was the best of all," Brown said. "We should have won the Super Bowl that year. We were the best team in the league. We were great in 1969. It still bugs me that we didn't win it all. That was our best chance."

NO RING TO IT

Carl Eller has four rings for winning the NFC championship. The rings are nice and shiny, but they don't satisfy him like the real thing would.

Yes, Eller would trade all four NFC championship rings for one piece of the elusive jewel: a Super Bowl ring.

"I regret not having won a Super Bowl," Eller said. "It was a big game and we played to win, but we couldn't."

Ironically, Eller said he believes the Vikings kept going back to the Super Bowl because they never won one. The pursuit kept the team hungry.

"I think, in truth, losing motivated us for a long time," Eller said. "We remained a dominant team for just about a decade, but I think it was that fire that propelled us to keep going until we could achieve it. We just weren't successful, but it wasn't because of a lack of effort."

BOOM BOOM

He's now known simply as Boom Boom. He's no longer Bill Brown. It's "Boom Boom Bill Brown."

"Everybody calls me Boom Boom," Brown said. "People I know call me Boom Boom and people I don't know call me Boom Boom."

Brown wasn't always so accepting of his moniker. Actually, he was appalled when a local newspaper writer stuck him with the nickname. In 1963, Brown's second season with the Vikings as a hard-nosed running back, the paper ran a picture of Brown running with the headline "Boom Boom Booms again."

"I guess it could be worse, I could be Boom Boom Boom," Brown said. "But two Booms is bad enough ... People really caught onto it and starting calling me 'Boom Boom.' I didn't like it at all."

Yet the name stuck. So Brown figured he better learn to live with it. So the following season, he started to respond when called Boom Boom.

"It's been nearly 40 years with Boom Boom," Brown said. "I guess I finally like it. After all, I now sign autographs as Boom Boom."

PARTY BOYS

Bill Brown said there was always something about the toughest guys on the team. They were always the wild children as well.

"The tougher the player, the wilder the guy," Brown summed. "It never failed. All of our tough guys loved to have a good time."

Brown said his toughest teammates were linebackers Roy Winston and Lonnie Warwick and quarterback Joe Kapp. They are all ornery players who gave it their all on the field. And all three gave it their all off the field.

"Partiers, the lot of them," Brown said. "I liked a good time, too, but those boys loved it. The team hung out at a bar called Eddie Webster's in Bloomington. Winston, Warwick and Kapp, they were the mayors of Eddie Webster's. If they weren't at practice, they were there. They were tough and wild."

ALMOST STREAK BUSTERS

For the past 30 years, the members of the 1972 Miami Dolphins have popped a bottle of champagne on the night the last undefeated team goes down. It's become an antici-pated occasion that is captured by television cameras.

After all, it's a wonderful reminder of one of the biggest achievements in NFL history. The 1972 Dolphins are the last NFL team to finish undefeated, at 17-0.

Yet if it wasn't for a gaffe by lovable Vikings' backup defensive end "Benchwarmer" Bob Lurtsema, the Dolphins wouldn't be popping the bubbly. Their greatness wouldn't be unique and it wouldn't have stood the test of time. They would have been just another team to lose a game.

On the third Sunday of the season, no one knew the Dolphins were going to end up perfect and win 14 more games in a row. On that day it just seemed like Miami dodged a major bullet.

Trailing late in the fourth quarter, the visiting Dolphins were stopped, sending the fans at the Met wild as they were celebrating what appeared to be the Vikings' second straight win after an opening season loss.

But Lurtsema was called for a controversial penalty, giving the Dolphins new life. They took advantage and scored the game-winning points in the final moments of the game, paving the way for a perfect season.

"I still get a lot of grief for that one," the man known as Lurtsy said. "I could have prevented history. If I only knew."

TOMMY KRAMER

Red McCombs was a Vikings fan long before he purchased the team in 1998. Even though McCombs was born and raised a Texan and the Dallas Cowboys were dominant in the 1970s and early '80s, McCombs and his family found themselves following the purple because of quarterback Tommy Kramer.

Like McCombs, Kramer is a native of San Antonio. Kramer was a Texas high school legend, and thousands in the San Antonio area used to go watch him under the Friday night lights.

McCombs was one of those who flocked to see schoolboy Tommy toss the pigskin.

"I've known Tommy for years," McCombs said.

"I was a real big Vikings fan because of Tommy. It's ironic that I later owned the team I watched so many times."

When the Vikings played a preseason game against New Orleans in San Antonio in 2001, Kramer was an honorary team captain and spent time again with McCombs.

*Tommy Kramer: Vikings owner Red McCombs was a
fan of Kramer when he was a schoolboy star in San Antonio.
(Photo courtesy of Rick Stewart/Getty Images)*

CHUCK FOREMAN

One of the players most respected by his teammates and coaches in Vikings history was running back Chuck Foreman.

On a team of stars, Foreman was sometimes overlooked. But ask anyone involved with the team and Foreman gets plenty of credit.

"What a horse," former offensive line coach John Michels said. "He absolutely carried us at times. Chuck was a load. It was a pleasure having my guys block for him. Chuck made it easy for all of us at times."

Foreman, whose career was slowed by injuries, played for the Vikings from 1973-79. Despite his relatively short time with the Vikings, he is second in franchise history, behind Robert Smith, in all-time yardage. He compiled 5,879 yards on 1,529 carries with the team.

"The thing about Chuck was he got better as the game went on," defensive end Bob Lurtsema said. "Chuck was nearly unstoppable in the fourth quarter. The other team would be tired and he was getting stronger. He just ran over people as the game wore on."

IS THAT REALLY YOU?

In the late 1970s, the Vikings players would often gather together in the evening for a night of music and socializing.

One night the group gathered at a friend of a player's apartment. It was the weekend and the team was getting lost. They weren't doing anything stupid, but the music got a tad loud. Up came a woman, knocking on the door. She was going to complain that the music was too loud. She went to the door in a robe and her hair in rollers.

Quarterback Tommy Kramer, one of the most visible players on the team, opened the door and greeted the woman warmly. She started reading him the riot act. He tried to calm her and told her he was Tommy Kramer and offered an autograph.

She laughed in his face. The woman told him she knew Tommy Kramer and he was no Tommy Kramer. After a few moments of a disagreement, another player came to the door.

The women said "Hey, you're a Viking. Then you must be Tommy Kramer then."

The woman rescinded her complaint and the party went on.

NEIGHBORHOOD FRIENDS

Jeff Diamond, an enterprising local kid, was an up-and-coming director of operations for the Vikings in 1978 when he was ordered by general manager Mike Lynn to go out and sign his first player to an NFL contract. The player Lynn assigned Diamond to rope was his close childhood friend Marc Trestman.

"Mike knew how close Marc and I were," Diamond recalled. "I brought the contract to Marc, he signed it, we laughed and we were both in the NFL. That deal took 10 seconds. I thought all contract negotiations were going to be like that."

Trestman's attempt at an NFL playing career didn't take, but since then, life in the NFL for the two kids from the Fernhill neighborhood in St. Louis Park has worked almost as perfectly as the plays they drew up together playing street football.

They worked together for two different stints with the Vikings. Diamond stayed with the team until 1999 and served in several capacities, ending up as the Vikings' senior vice president of football operations. Trestman was a Vikings offensive assistant coach from 1985-86 and '90-91.

The lifelong friends would love to reunite again.

"I don't know how many times we talked about me being the president of a team and he being the head coach," Diamond said. "It's our dream. I'd love to work with Marc. I know someday he is going to make a great head coach. Just like we always talked."

Chapter 2

One Offensive Line

THE CHEWER

For four decades, Vikings offensive linemen have had the unmistakable pleasure of entering the world of John Michels. The offensive line coach was with the team from 1967-93, making him the longest-tenured coach in team history.

Michels spent four decades giving many, many earfuls—or, as Michels himself put it, "butt chewing."

"I love to give butt chewings," Michels said proudly. "Every player I ever coached all got plenty of butt chewing. I'd yell at everyone and anyone. That's the way I did it. After a while, players knew it wasn't personal. They just expected it."

Michels thought expressing himself vocally and loudly was the best way of teaching. Plus, it was nothing new for the Vikings. After all, when Michels joined Bud Grant's first staff in 1967, they replaced Norm Van Brocklin, who was well known for his own brand of "butt chewing."

"Guys weren't that impressed with me," Michels said with a chuckle. "They were coming off Van Brocklin, who was the master butt chewer. They'd say to me, 'You're nothing. We had the Dutchman. We're ready for you.' But I still think I had my own kind of butt chewing that made me special, too."

MICK TINGELHOFF

When John Michels joined the Vikings coaching staff in 1967 under Bud Grant, he knew all about Mick Tingelhoff, the scrappy center. Tingelhoff was already established when Michels came on the scene. So Michels was excited to get a chance to work with Tingelhoff.

His impressions: "The toughest guy I ever coached," Michels said. "Everything I heard about was true. This guy was just a warrior. You didn't want to tangle with Mick Tingelhoff."

Tingelhoff had the desire that Michels had never seen before. There were many games in which Tingelhoff was so battered he shouldn't have played. But he never missed a game.

"There was one game when his leg was basically just hanging there," Michels said. "I told Mick he wasn't going to play. He looked at me and said, 'Forget about it. I'm playing.' You know what? He went on and just clobbered his opponent. Mick was just the toughest guy I knew."

RANDALL McDANIEL

Randall McDaniel was a first-round draft pick. Mick Tingelhoff went undrafted. That's where the differences between the two ended for John Michels.

Eleven years after Tingelhoff retired, Michels was able to work with a player who most reminded him of Tingelhoff. Like Tingelhoff, McDaniel was a powerful guard who didn't say much. He just quietly went about his work.

Also like Tingelhoff, McDaniel was tough and dominated his opponents.

"Randall was a young Mick," Michels said. "He wouldn't say boo to you but he'd beat you down."

There wasn't a player Michels had since Tingelhoff retired who worked as hard as he did—until McDaniel came into town.

"Mick liked to tangle and so did Randall," Michels said. "If you went after Randall on the field, he'd come right at you and was ready to fight until one of you were dead. And my money was always on Randall, just like it was with Mick."

RON YARY

John Michels coached several star athletes, but Ron Yary was simply the best. The Hall of Famer, Michels said, possessed a unique combination of athletic ability, strength, intelligence, toughness and nastiness. Oh boy, did Yary have some nastiness in him.

"That man had a mean streak on the field," Michels said. "He literally wanted to destroy his opponent. He took it so personally and wanted to dismantle his opponent. And in most cases, Ron was successful."

Michels said the biggest key with Yary was making sure he was calm enough. Yary was the excitable type.

"He couldn't wait to get on the field and tear people apart," Michels said. "Ron was sky high. You tried to calm him, but it was a challenge. He wanted to get on the field and use that nastiness."

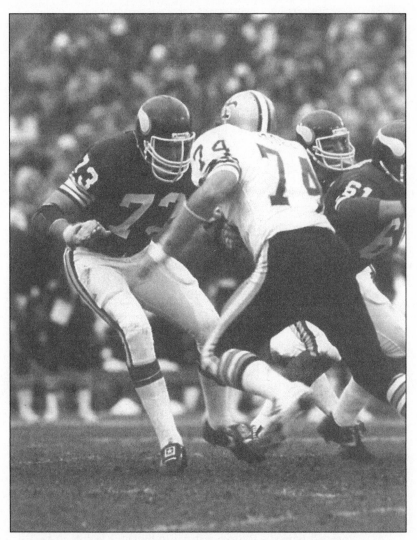

Ron Yary: The Hall of Fame left tackle was tough during games and practices. He had a nasty mean streak and was also a great technician. (Photo by Rick A. Kolodziej)

HONORING A FRIEND

When Ron Yary finally made it into the Hall of Fame in January, 2001, a former teammate was at the announcement on Super Bowl weekend in Tampa, Florida.

"I had to be here for it," said former Vikings defensive end Bob Lurtsema said. "Ronny really deserved this. I went against so many offensive linemen in my career, but Ronny was the best."

Lurtsema said Yary made all of his teammates better.

"Practicing against Ron Yary was practicing against the best," Lurtsema said. "Getting blocked by him was an honor. You just knew you were competing against the best. That's why he deserved to be a Hall of Famer and I'm proud to be there for it."

FINALLY MADE IT

It had gotten to the point where Ron Yary would only halfheartedly fantasize about standing at the podium in Canton, Ohio. His chances were waning.

Thanks to a grass-roots campaign by the organization he anchored with toughness and competitiveness, he allowed himself to believe perhaps it would happen. In January, 2001, it did happen. Yary, the Vikings' right tackle on four Super Bowl teams, became the franchise's sixth member of the Hall of Fame.

Voters credited a strong campaign by the Vikings in favor of Yary, who played for Minnesota from 1968-81. The campaign was led by Yary's coach, Bud Grant, and Vikings owner Red McCombs, who bought the team three years ago.

"In recent years, I didn't pay close attention to it, but this year I was hoping it would happen," said Yary, voted into the shrine in his 14th year of eligibility. After 15 years of eligibility, players become senior nominees. Only one senior nominee is eligible for election every year. Yary was one of 15 finalists.

"There was a nice push for me, and I really appreciate it," he said. "Now that I've made it, I'm just elated. It's an unreal feeling."

Grant, a 1994 inductee, deflected credit for helping get Yary elected.

"Ron earned it. He did it himself," he said. "Ron was one of the great competitors I coached. Ron simply liked to play football. You never had to motivate Ron. He always wanted to be the best, and he was."

YARY WAS A TRUE VIKING

Yary, the Vikings' first-round draft pick in 1968 from the University of Southern California, embodied the personality of Bud Grant's teams. He was agile, bright, and aggressive—and he hated to lose. He missed only two games before being traded to his hometown Los Angeles Rams in 1982 for his 15th and final season.

Yary was chosen for the Pro Bowl seven times and was the anchor of the offensive line of four Super Bowl teams. Many credit Yary for creating the scrambling of quarterback Fran Tarkenton.

"Fran wouldn't have been the runner he was without Ron opening up huge holes," former Vikings defensive end

Bob Lurtsema said. "Ron was a great pulling tackle. He had great moves. The thing about Ron was he was more focused on football and winning than anyone I played with. He lived for football. He'd get upset when other people weren't as focused on football as he was. ... I hated practicing against him because he was so into football all the time, even in practice. He was brutal to play against."

NO REGRETS

Many defensive opponents considered Ron Yary a mean, nasty player. He was tough and unforgiving.

But Yary had no regrets over how he approached the game. Football was Yary's passion.

"I loved every minute of it. I loved being around my teammates," he said. "I loved winning. It was the greatest thing in the world. ... But when you lost, it was the worst occupation in the world."

Yary retired with his family in Southern California, where he headed a successful construction company.

GARY ZIMMERMAN

There are no questions amongst the men who coached Gary Zimmerman—he belongs in the Hall of Fame.

"There's no question in my mind, Gary is a Hall of Famer," said John Michels, who was Zimmerman's offensive line coach with the Vikings. "Gary is the best technician I've ever seen as an offensive lineman. It's hard to say an offensive lineman dominated. But Gary dominated nearly every player he ever faced."

Zimmerman joined the Vikings in 1986 after playing in the short-lived USFL. Zimmerman then joined Denver in 1993 and finished his career with the Broncos.

"I remember him as about as good an offensive lineman as I've ever seen," former Vikings head coach Jerry Burns said. "He wasn't the biggest lineman in the league, but he was smart, sound and just plain excellent. He deserves to be in the Hall."

THE WHITE ELEPHANT

Ed White was a gigantic animal. Make that an extremely nice gigantic animal.

"Ed was this huge elephant," said his line coach John Michels. "That's the first thing that pops into my head about Ed. He was an elephant. That's what I always thought to myself: 'Ed White is this huge elephant.'"

Michels's trick, though, was making the amiable White a true king of the jungle. Michels thought White was simply too nice when he joined the team. But Michels, who prided himself in making his players nasty, finally worked his will with White.

After a while, White turned surly and started using his great size to his advantage. He ended up being one of the best offensive linemen in team history.

"Ed got meaner and the elephant started hurting people," Michels said. "I was very proud that the gigantic elephant turned into a mean hunter."

THE UNDERRATED ONE

In 27 seasons with the Vikings, John Michels coached hundreds of offensive linemen.

He saw them all—from Ron Yary to Mick Tingelhoff to Randall McDaniel to Gary Zimmerman. He coached many stars and had the pleasure of being around several great players. But one of the most memorable players he's ever been associated with is the unheralded Grady Alderman. The gritty tackle played for the Vikings from 1961-74.

"Coaching Grady is one of the most memorable parts of my career," Michels said. "Not many people give him credit but he was really the glue to those great lines."

Michels said the best part of coaching Alderman was that he never needed to actually be coached. Alderman—a certified public accountant—was so smart, he didn't require much attention.

"He was one of the easiest players I ever coached," Michels said. "I never had to tell him anything. He was like having an extra coach on the field."

BLOCKING FOR TARKENTON

One of the most difficult parts of John Michels's duties as the Vikings' offensive line coach was having his players adjust to the wild ways of quarterback Fran Tarkenton.

There was just no planning for Tarkenton's famous fits of the runs. He'd take off scrambling at anytime and his linemen would have no clue.

Yet Michels told his players to stay within the plan and not run off course trying to save their scrambling quarterback. There was no way he'd allow his linemen to freelance along with their gambling signal caller.

"When Fran took off he was on his own and he knew that," Michels said. "It was part of the deal. If I had my guys take off with him it would be pure anarchy and then we'd all be in trouble."

Still, Michels said having the scrambling Tarkenton on his side was more of a pleasure than a difficulty.

"He'd cause us trouble every game with that scrambling of his," Michels said. "He'd drive us a little crazy, but he drove the opposition even crazier. So we loved the scrambler."

GREAT COMPETITION

One of John Michels's career highlights came during the 1970s when the Vikings had perhaps the best defensive line ever assembled. You know the crew—Jim Marshall, Carl Eller, Alan Page and Gary Larsen. The group is better known as the Purple People Eaters, one of the greatest and well-known monikers in all of sports.

Michels also felt pretty good about his offensive line, which included Hall of Famer Ron Yary and stars Mick Tingelhoff and Ed White. Even though the offensive line was star-studded, it didn't get nearly the amount of publicity as the much-ballyhooed defensive line.

Michels admitted it. He and his players took it personally.

"We loved our defensive line, but they got all the press," Michels said. "We thought we were pretty good, too."

The results were some ultra-competitive practice sessions.

The Purple People Eaters: (Left to right) Jim Marshall, Alan Page,
Gary Larsen, Carl Eller. Dominant as a group and stars in their
own right, these guys were the face of the Vikings in the '70s.
(Photo by Rick A. Kolodziej)

"Oh man, did we go at it," Michels said. "I think our
practices were harder than some games. We wanted to make
our point, and so our linemen would really make the Purple
People Eaters work for their money. That's why they were
so good. They had great competition every day at practice.
Those were two great lines doing battle on a daily basis."

GREAT INDIVIDUALS

It's ironic. One of the greatest collections of defensive
linemen to ever play together was so great because of the
individual talent that composed the unit.

"They all played great together, but they were all great as individuals," said Bob Lurtsema, a backup defensive lineman who had the pleasure of playing behind the Purple People Eaters.

The vaunted 1970s Vikings defensive line—composed of Jim Marshall, Carl Eller, Alan Page and Gary Larsen—is still considered one of the greatest lines ever put together.

"Any one of those four players would have been stars had they played without the other two," offensive line coach John Michels said. "Together, they were known as one. But they were all monsters. Just monsters. You'll never see a group like that play together again. It's been more than 25 years and no group has ever gotten close to the Purple People Eaters, and no group ever will."

THE OTHER PURPLE PEOPLE EATER

Gary Larsen was like the fourth tenor.

Larsen was the fourth member of the famed Purple People Eaters. Yet many folks have a hard time remembering his name. That's what happens when you're part of a conglomerate that includes the likes of Hall of Famer Alan Page and fellow Minnesota legends Jim Marshall and Carl Eller.

You kind of get lost in the shuffle. But those who knew Larsen said he was much more than an afterthought.

"Gary belonged with the greatness of the Purple People Eaters," backup defensive lineman Bob Lurtsema said. "He truly belonged."

Coach John Michels admitted Larsen wasn't as fast or athletically gifted as the more famous People Eaters, but he was a great fit with the group. He complemented his linemates well.

"Gary did a lot of cleaning up for those guys," Michels said. "They'd start the play and he'd help finish it up. Gary never let anything get past him. He was like a giant vacuum cleaner. He picked up the pieces."

SACK ARTIST

Defensive end Carl Eller considered himself an artist on the field. Of course, the great Eller painted his way into Vikings lore by being, ahem, a sack artist.

Eller, already a Minnesota legend from his days as a collegiate Gopher, etched his way into Vikings history with a team-high 130 sacks.

A historian who studied great artists, Eller said he worked at his craft as if he was composing rare, breathtaking artwork that would stand the test of time and never go out of style.

"I don't know if guys like Rembrandt or Michelangelo or Picasso worked with the thought that they would be the best at what they did. I don't think that when they did their masterpieces like the Mona Lisa or the Sistine Chapel that they thought it would be something people would appreciate years after they were gone. That's how I approached the game. The testament to me is that people do remember the way I played.

"A lot of people think I was the best who ever played. I hear that a lot. I feel like I was one of the best players to ever play the position and with that I take satisfaction knowing that when I played, I worked very hard at my craft and people enjoyed the way I played."

Chapter 3

The Coaches

THE NORM VAN BROCKLIN DAYS

Norm Van Brocklin, the former star quarterback, was the Vikings' coach for their first six years of existence. Those six years weren't fun days for the players, especially in training camp.

Van Brocklin was a big believer in the no-pain no-gain philosophy. So training camps were predictability brutal. Water was forbidden during practice, and the Dutchman was known for cutting a player he was particularly disgusted with right there on the practice field.

"Norm would undress guys right in front of everyone," running back Bill Brown said.

"He'd yell at guys pretty good. I saw many of my buddies get yelled at by Norm."

Because talent was so thin in the early years, everyday Joes such as bartenders, truck drivers and mailmen would show up to training camp in the mosquito-riddled woods of Bemidji.

"Those were tough days," star center Mick Tingelhoff said.

"Days were long and Norm was very hard on us."

Brown said the combination of Van Brocklin's tactics and the elements of Bemidji made training camp a difficult place to be. Bemidji would get cold and rainy in the summer.

Still, the weather didn't matter to Van Brocklin. He'd practice the team up to six hours a day in training camp. As a reward for making it through a long day of camp, Van Brocklin would have the team do a series of wind sprints as dessert.

"Norm would have us out in it whether it was hot or cold," Brown said. "He'd run us all day and we've be dripping wet some days. Those really were the days, boy."

THE BUD GRANT DAYS

Unlike the seven years under Van Brocklin, new coach Bud Grant brought a steady heartbeat to the program. Unlike Van Brocklin, Grant was under control and rarely raised his voice. His new players instantly took to it. The new style translated into instant results on the field.

Grant, who turned out to be one of the most legendary coaches in NFL history, had his players behind him from the start. While the Vikings won just three games in Grant's first season, the team believed in their new coach, and he had them on the right track. The next season, the Vikings finished better than .500 and advanced to the playoffs for the first time in team history. They were on the fast track to becoming one of the elite teams in the NFL.

The players praised Grant because they always knew where they stood with him.

Bud Grant: The Hall of Famer—considered the best coach never to win the Super Bowl—turned the Vikings into a perennial contender. (Photo by Rick A. Kolodziej)

"Bud didn't take any garbage, but he didn't overdo it, either," running back Bill Brown said. "He wouldn't overwork you, but he did expect his players to work hard while we were on the practice field."

The best part of Grant, according to Brown, was the native Minnesotan's even keel.

"We were used to Norm Van Brocklin's yelling and screaming, and Bud was a man of few words," Brown said. "Everything was the same with Bud. Whether it was the first game of the season or the Super Bowl, Bud pretty much had the same thing to say. He'd tell us we had our work cut out for us and to play smart. We appreciated it and it showed."

COULDN'T FOOL BUD

It wasn't uncommon for a player to occasionally miss curfew during training camp.

One night of camp, reveling got particularly late for defensive end Bob Lurtsema, and he broke the 11 p.m. curfew. So he had to sneak back into the team's dormitory.

The next morning, Lurtsema thought he was in the clear. He was sure he made it back to his room unnoticed. However, the word got around that coach Bud Grant—a stickler for rules and regulations—had caught wind that some players were burning the midnight oil, and they weren't doing it by studying their playbook.

Lurtsema immediately became nervous when he heard Grant knew something was up. Paranoia overtook his huge body.

"I went out on the practice field and could just feel Coach Grant looking at me," Lurtsema said. "I told my buddies he knew it was me."

So, feeling guilty, Lurtsema worked his heart out during practice trying to make up for his miscues. But actually working hard was his mistake.

"Bud saw me working harder than everything else and knew I had something to hide," Lurtsema said. "That's how he found out it was me who broke curfew. Bud did it again. He won out in the mental game. He always did. That's what made Bud so great and that's what made me so dumb."

STILL ON THE PAYROLL

Bud Grant is Minnesota. He's hard-working, honest, and rugged.

So the native Minnesotan who became the most loved and famous member of the Vikings' organization that he coached for three decades obviously remained a major part of the franchise and the state in his retirement.

Grant remains employed by the Vikings as a consultant. He spends part of the day at the office—the part in which he's not hunting and fishing.

"After football, being an outdoorsman became my life," Grant said. "I can't get enough of being at my cabin. I love my work, but I love fishing and hunting a little more these days."

THE LES STECKEL DAYS

Les Steckel, a former Marine, replaced Bud Grant in 1984 for one year. It was one long year, in which Steckel was nationally renowned for running yearlong boot camp.

Steckel was certainly a disciple of the Norm Van Brocklin way of coaching. He brought the Iron Man Challenge to the camp. Players would have to perform a series of running and weightlifting exercises in a predetermined elapsed time.

The players did not buy into Steckel's controversial tactics, and the season was a disaster as they went 3-13.

Some players most remember Steckel for his self-inflicted pain. To fire the team up before facing Green Bay in Milwaukee, Steckel inexplicably punched himself in the face.

The knockout didn't work. The Packers punched the Vikings in the face, 45-17.

Jerry Burns: The lovable longtime coach was known for his quirks, superstitions, and fears. Show Burns a rodent and watch him jump on his desk.
(Photo by Rick A. Kolodziej)

JERRY BURNS

Jerry Burns was extremely superstitious. Actually, he was downright strange at times.

But players loved Burns, who was the Vikings' longtime offensive coordinator before becoming head coach for six years. Players got to know Burns's quirks well, and they occasionally took advantage of them.

Burns's two biggest superstitions involved coins and animals. He'd always pick up coins for good luck. Well, make that he'd always pick up coins that were heads up for good luck. He'd avoid coins with the tails showing.

When it came to animals, though, Burns steered clear. He was especially afraid of mice and snakes.

Before games players would plant coins—heads up— for Burns to pick up. Some days, his back would hurt because he was picking up so many coins.

The other tricks the players played on their coach weren't so financially productive for Burns.

"These guys would put mice near Jerry and even put snakes in his desk," Jeff Diamond said, still laughing at the memory.

"And I don't think they were toy snakes."

DENNIS GREEN: A PROUD BRANCH

Dennis Green was a proud branch of the Bill Walsh tree.

Green, an assistant for Walsh during the dynasty days of the San Francisco 49ers of the early 1980s, loved to make analogies and talk about his mentor, Bill Walsh. The combination made for a comical explanation.

Green believes the Walsh connection will never end. The influence of the coach who built the San Francisco 49ers into an NFL dynasty, Green said, is deeply rooted throughout the league.

Green waited for the next generation of Walsh coaching babies to be born. The family extended when former Baltimore assistants Marvin Lewis (Cincinnati) and Jack Del Rio (Jacksonville) became head coaches for the 2003 season. Brian Billick was head coach with the Ravens. Billick was a Vikings assistant coach for Green for seven seasons before graduating to head coach in Baltimore.

"The tree will never stop," Green said. "That makes me very proud."

ALL IN THE FAMILY

In 2001, Dennis Green and his son Jeremy made NFL history. They became the first father-son trading partners.

In addition to being the Vikings coach, Dennis Green was also the vice president of football operations. Jeremy Green was in the personnel department with Cleveland. As the two talked—like most fathers and sons, Dennis and Jeremy spoke several times a week on the phone—often their chats would lead to work, which led to discussing players on each team, which in turn led to talking turkey.

So in 2001, over the span of two months, the father and son ended their conversations by making two trades. First, the Vikings acquired steady offensive lineman Everett Lindsay from the Browns. Then in later swaps they picked up running back Travis Prentice and quarterback Spergon Wynn and then later received defensive end Stalin Colinet from the Browns. The Vikings sent draft picks in every trade.

Dennis Green: There is a Dennis Green tree of coaching in the NFL.
Several of his former assistants are now head coaches themselves.
(Photo by Rick A. Kolodziej)

*Brian Billick: The former offensive coordinator
was an innovator when it came to using computer
technology. His office looked like a space station.
(Photo by Rick A. Kolodziej)*

"I think we made history," Dennis Green said. "It's unusual [that a] father and son makes trades. It was fun."

FAMILY TIME

Dennis Green had a ritual every Friday during the season: He'd go fishing with his wife Marie and their two small children.

Fishing was Green's greatest passion. He started the passion with his wife and wanted to introduce the sport to his kids.

On Fridays before games, Green was routinely out of the office by 2 p.m. and the family would hit a local lake for an afternoon of boat fishing.

"It's relaxing," Green said. "It's gets me ready for the game."

BRIAN BILLICK

When Brian Billick's Baltimore Ravens won the 2000 Super Bowl in his second season as head coach, Billick gave much praise and credit to his mentor, Dennis Green. Billick was the Vikings' offensive coordinator under Green and coached for him at Stanford.

While Billick credits Green for giving him his start, everyone involved with the Vikings knew Billick was a coaching star in the making.

Billick was the mastermind behind the Vikings' record-breaking offense in 1998. He had a unique knack of getting everything out of the Vikings' varied offensive weapons. The Vikings confused teams on the run and with the pass.

Billick relied on computer technology for his madness. His office looked like a space station, and he was known as one of the first coaches in the NFL to utilize computers.

"Brian was at the cutting edge of technology," Tice said. "He knew there was a technological game within the game. I learned so much about the inner workings of studies and computer usage from Brian."

MORE TECHNOLOGY

Because Brian Billick relied so much on computers and technology, he was in close contact with Mike Eayrs, who was the team's computer analyst for several years. Eayrs was a vital part of the team in the 1990s. He was in charge of computing statistics and trends and tendencies of not only the Vikings, but their opponents as well.

The Vikings' coaching staff was always quick to credit Eayrs for his contribution. In fact, when defensive coordinator Tony Dungy left to become the head coach in Tampa Bay and when Billick left for Baltimore, they both tried to sway Eayrs away.

Eayrs did finally leave the team to go to rival Green Bay prior to the 2001 season. The Vikings undoubtedly missed Eayrs, especially since he went to a division rival. But because he was with the team so long, the Vikings knew what to expect from him as well.

In the Vikings' first game against the Packers and Eayrs in 2001, the Vikings pounded Green Bay. It was almost as if they knew what the Packers were doing.

"We turned the tables on Mike," laughed an assistant coach. "Technology is a great thing. But we knew what Mike was going to be looking for in us and we changed our game plan. It backfired on him. Mike helped us win many games with his information. We miss him. But we weren't going to let him outsmart us once he left us."

SOME SENSE OF HUMOR

The loss to the Atlanta Falcons in the 1998 NFC championship game will go down as one of the most disappointing, devastating days in Vikings history. After all, it appeared during the magical 1998 run that the Vikings were a team of destiny. It appeared they were on their way to the first Super Bowl championship in team history and the first Super Bowl appearance in two decades.

They were the best team in the NFL with a startling 15-1 record and shattered league scoring records. They were simply super.

But then it all fell apart when upstart Atlanta came into the Metrodome and stunned the Vikings in overtime. The loss was devastating to the Vikings. They thought about the loss all off season, making the cold Minnesota winter all the more bitter.

The Vikings wanted to forget that game and to forget about the Falcons. So what happened? In their first game of the next season, the Vikings opponent was none other than the Atlanta Falcons. Green didn't chuckle at the scheduling, which he said wasn't ironic.

"The NFL has quite a sense of humor," Green said. "They sent us to play the Falcons in the first game after the NFC championship game. I didn't see the humor."

GREAT COLLEGE TRAINING

Before he began his 10-season run as the Vikings' coach, Green was the head coach at Stanford. Over the years in the NFL, Green would come across several players he recruited to The Farm and coached there. One of his favorite NFL players was special teams ace and backup receiver Chris Walsh. The player followed Green from Stanford to the Vikings.

"I love Chris Walsh. He got great college coaching," Green joked.

That was his favorite line when he'd run across a player he coached at Stanford. When the Vikings played Tampa Bay and safety John Lynch, Green would dust off his favorite line.

"John Lynch is a great player. It's because of his great college training," Green would deadpan.

IRON MEN

Dennis Green was loved by the people who worked for him. He took care of them if they did their jobs.

If you worked hard in Green's world, he'd be extremely loyal and rewarding to you. The shining example of Green's goodness to his employees was his Iron Man award.

A player, coach, training staff member or support staff member who was able to participate in every training camp practice was given the Iron Man award. Green began the incentive system his first year as the Vikings' coach.

He'd reward the Iron Men with different electronic gifts each year. The longer a person was in the Vikings camp and the more Iron Men camps he'd complete, the better the re-ward. Prizes ranged from small stereos to 32-inch televi-sions.

"I had to get a whole new home entertaining center because of that man," said Sammy Casalenda, a longtime employee. "He treated us real nice."

Green's good deeds rubbed off on his successor, Mike Tice. Tice, an assistant under Green, continued the Iron Men tradition when he became head coach.

TEAM QUARTERBACK

Dennis Green prided himself in making the Vikings a quarterback-making factory. No matter who was the quar-terback of the team, they succeeded.

"It's the system," Green said. "We have a very quarter-back-friendly system. Quarterbacks succeed in our system."

Green proudly manufactured several quality quarter-backs. In the 2002 season, former Vikings quarterback Rich Gannon was named the NFL MVP. Plus, Minnesota signal callers Brad Johnson (Tampa Bay) and Jay Fiedler (Miami) enjoyed great success.

"I learned a lot in Minnesota," Johnson said. "A lot of great quarterbacks came out of there. Being there helped my career."

LISTENING TO BUD

The 2002 season was tough for Mike Tice, in his first season as Vikings head coach. He wasn't used to losing. Tice had always won in every aspect of his career, whether it was a player or as an assistant coach.

But in his first season as a coach, the 43-year-old started 0-4 and admitted he needed some reassurance and encouragement.

He didn't have to look far—or walk far, for that matter. All Tice had to do was stroll down the hallway to see former coach and current consultant Bud Grant.

If anyone knew what Tice was feeling and how to deal with it, it was Grant. In his first season as the Vikings' coach in 1967 as a 40-year-old, Grant's team won just three games. And, of course, Grant's tenure turned out just fine.

"Bud was a Godsend for me," Tice said. "Many, many Monday mornings that first year were spent in his office. He was a huge help. He told me just to be myself and to believe in my program. If it's coming from Bud Grant, I'm listening. I'm glad he's a Viking."

GEORGE O'LEARY

How many NFL head coaches have someone around their team who was around for their first date, their first pimple, their first trip to detention?

Well, Mike Tice did. And it was even by choice.

On his first day as the Vikings' head coach, Tice hired George O'Leary as his defensive line coach. O'Leary later became the Vikings' defensive coordinator. Tice wanted to surround himself with people who truly knew him. O'Leary certainly qualified.

O'Leary coached Tice and his younger brother John at Central Islip High School on Long Island, New York in the 1970s. Tice was the quarterback of the team.

"I know that kid from way back," O'Leary said. "I knew his family and I knew everything about him. It's funny how life takes certain turns, but it's great to be with Mike. He's come a long way since he was 15."

NO NAP TIME

Pete Bercich became a Vikings defensive assistant coach in 2002, two years after his seven-year playing career with the team ended.

He sandwiched his time with the Vikings as a player and as a coach with nearly two years in private business. Obviously, he was thrilled to be back in the game, "talking about football with my family every day."

But even though he was back with the team, Bercich quickly realized there was a difference between being a player and a coach, especially at training camp.

The players got a long break in between the morning and afternoon practice, long enough for them to take a nice, lengthy nap. However, coaches met and watched film in between practice sessions.

"I miss that nap," Bercich said. "That's the biggest difference. I tell all my former teammates they're so lucky to get that nap."

Chapter 4

Training Camp

RUN WITH HERD

It was his first training camp with the Vikings, and journeyman defensive end Bob Lurtsema was trying to impress the coaching staff. After all, he was trying to win a spot on the line that featured the famed Purple People Eaters.

Lurtsema wasn't going to let up.

He thought he was doing the right thing after sprinting as fast as he could during a post-practice running session. Lurtsema broke past his linemates, showing his energy and spirit.

It was the last time he broke from the pack. Defensive end Jim Marshall, the leader of the unit, didn't take kindly to Lurtsema going out on his own while the rest of the linemen gingerly completed the workout.

"I ran past and Jim yelled—I'll never forget it—'Don't be a turd, run with the herd,'" Lurtsema said. "I thought he was joking."

But Marshall wasn't. He wanted his teammates to run together.

At lunchtime, the two went at it again. They went on the roof of the team's dorm at Mankato State, Gage Hall. Millard and Kiffin had already made amends and were on good terms again. But they decided to have a little fun.

On the roof, with several people milling below, the two began mockingly yelling at each other. It caught everyone's attention below. Then, Millard suddenly stepped back and Kiffin tossed below a dummy made out of a mattress. As it hurtled to the ground, it became apparent it had Millard's jersey on it.

Some witnesses were startled, watching the purple-clad dummy crash to the ground. Once everyone realized it was a mattress and not Millard who took flight, they looked up and saw the player and coach laughing.

CHILD'S PLAY

Daunte Culpepper and Randy Moss are, obviously, two tough men. They are rugged, physical athletes, who happen to love their cartoons.

The star quarterback and his go-to wide receiver are easy to spot at training camp—they are the ones with the Scooby Doo. Both players walk around during camp with backpacks featuring depictions of the cartoon on them. Yes, pro football players—Pro Bowl players, at that—tote their playbooks in the same backpack a seven-year-old would carry his coloring books and Pokemon cards in.

Yet Culpepper and Moss are far from embarrassed. In fact, Culpepper brought Scooby Doo sheets to camp and Moss wears Scooby Doo sweaters.

"I love cartoons," Culpepper said. "I don't care who knows it. I'm a kid at heart; Randy is too."

Daunte Culpepper: The huge quarterback is a child at heart. It's not unusual to see him sporting a backpack featuring his favorite cartoon character—Scooby Doo. (Photo by Rick A. Kolodziej)

CAMP RIDES

The key for players during training camp is to reserve as much energy as possible. After all, the players wake at 6 a.m. and are working all the way up to 11 p.m. with two long practices and countless meetings in between. So the days are tiring.

With practice, weight training, meeting rooms and the dorms all blocks away from each other at Minnesota State-Mankato, players spend a lot of their day simply walking.

Not all players, though. Many bring their own bikes or rent bikes at the school for the three-week camp.

There have been other modes of transportation. Some players have brought skateboards and defensive back Ronnie Bradford even brought a motorized scooter.

"I use this every camp," the industrious Bradford said of the crude, homemade rig. "I have to save my legs."

Quarterback Daunte Culpepper shunned the comforts of the mountain bike most players favored. Instead, Culpepper brought a bright orange dirt bike. The small bike looked like it would comfortably accommodate a seventh grader. The six-foot-four, 260-pound Culpepper was a tight fit, but he loved it.

"I always wanted one of these," Culpepper said. "I think I look great on it."

Chapter 5

Moss and Carter

THE NFL'S MOST DANGEROUS PLAYER

Randy Moss showed his uncanny versatility in a two-minute sequence against Miami on December 21, 2002.

In the first drive of the fourth quarter, Moss displayed why he is the NFL's most dangerous player, and he did it with both his hands and his arms.

With the Vikings trailing 14-10, quarterback Daunte Culpepper hit Moss in single coverage for a 60-yard catch, giving the Vikings the ball at the Dolphins' 10. It came on a crucial third down and 14 play from their own 30-yard line.

The huge play set up an even more significant play.

Moss then threw a 13-yard touchdown pass to fellow receiver D'Wayne Bates to give the Vikings a 17-14 lead with 11:53 remaining in the game. It was Moss's second career touchdown pass, having thrown a would-be victorious touchdown pass in the final seconds to quarterback Daunte Culpepper earlier in the season against Atlanta.

*Randy Moss: The Pro Bowl wide receiver is considered by
many as the best player in the NFL. He's so athletic
that he rarely has to stretch before games and practices.
(Photo by Rick A. Kolodziej)*

However, the play was called back because of illegal formation, and the Falcons eventually won the game in overtime.

A week later, there was nothing illegal about this reverse pass. But it wasn't easy.

Miami's left end Adewale Ogunleye sniffed out the play and closed in on Moss. However, Moss was able to spin away from his pursuer. Moss then threw a perfect strike to Bates, who shook his coverage to make the catch.

"[Ogunleye] came up and made the play, but Randy, being the athlete that he is, made a bigger play," Culpepper said. "He made [Ogunleye] miss and threw it behind D'Wayne on purpose because he was covered. Moss had a great play."

Vikings Offensive coordinator Scott Linehan said those two plays illustrate Moss's talents.

"He's a big-play player," Linehan said. "He's a go-to guy. Whether it's 60 yards, three yards, a reverse pass. Whenever you need Randy, he is there. It's his versatility that makes him the best."

THE BEST

Randy Moss is arguably the most athletic player in the NFL. He does things that leave even the most experienced and most ardent NFL observers gape-mouthed on a weekly basis.

He leaps higher than most players, his hands are as sure as any player in the league, and his getaway speed is as fast as any player in the league. But perhaps the best evidence of Moss's superior athleticism comes before the Sunday juices are flowing and before the bright lights of the cameras are on.

Moss displays what a great athlete he is before every practice. As does every NFL team, the Vikings conduct a tedious but necessary 10-15 minute stretching process directly before practice begins every day. Every player carefully performs the exercises to loosen up for practice and to insure against injuries.

While the rest of his teammates are on the ground stretching, Moss usually stands up, jogging in place. Moss is so superior he requires little if any stretching prior to going to work. Occasionally, he stretches momentarily, but often he just stands and plays catch with an equipment manager.

"Randy is special and different," Mike Tice said. "He comes ready."

GREEN BAY NIGHT

It was the night 20 NFL teams realized what a horrible mistake they had made. There was already proof that Randy Moss was a star in the making, but his star was undeniably shining after he went into Lambeau Field and crippled the Packers.

This was the same Green Bay team that was coming off two straight Super Bowl appearances. This was the same Lambeau Field that was a prison for most opponents.

But under the national spotlight of Monday night, Randy Moss crumbled the Lambeau Field lore. During the 1998 season, in just his fifth NFL game, Moss had 190 yards on five catches with two touchdowns.

Moss brought in bombs all night as the Vikings pounded the Packers 37-24 in a constant rainstorm. Moss put away any doubt that he was going to be a star in the NFL.

"Randy arrived that night," Dennis Green said. "In a big way."

DOG OR DAWG?

Randy Moss's favorite greeting has always been "What's up, Dawg?" Surfers have their "dude," farmers have their "howdy" and Moss has his "dawg."

Moss refers to everyone as "dawg," whether it's a teammate, an opponent, a coach or a reporter.

Vikings coach Mike Tice remembers his first practice as the interim head coach on the afternoon Dennis Green was fired in January 2002. During the practice, Moss suddenly came over to Tice and expressed his support to the new coach.

"'I've got your back, Dawg,'" Tice remembered Moss telling him. "That was his way of saying he accepted me. I was his Dawg."

Tice, who was already close to Moss as an assistant coach, continued to be the top Dawg. Moss usually called Tice every Tuesday, the players' off day, during the season.

"The phone would ring, and I'd hear, 'What's up Dawg?' on the other end," Tice said. "I automatically knew it was Randy. He's my Dawg."

FOOLING THE ENEMY

Every Wednesday, local media conduct a conference call with an opposing player. Traditionally, one of the most entertaining teleconferences is held with loquacious Tampa Bay defensive tackle Warren Sapp. He is always the overwhelming choice for the conference. These calls can often be stale and boring, but Sapp always offers honest and colorful responses.

In 2001, the call got downright juicy when Vikings receiver Randy Moss made a spontaneous appearance in the media room, joining surprised reporters for their call.

When Sapp got on the line, Moss jumped in with a loud and obnoxious, "Mr. Sapp, Mr. Sapp."

"Yeah," said an annoyed and unexpecting Sapp.

"How are you going to stop Randy Moss?" asked Moss, trying to hold back his laughter.

"We're not concentrating on Randy Moss. He's part of the team we want to stop," retorted Sapp, obviously upset by the tone of the question.

Moss couldn't hold it in any longer. And neither could the 10 reporters in the room. Moss stopped the charade and said, cracking up, "Hey, Dawg, it's me." Sapp immediately erupted into laughter.

"That boy is crazy," Sapp said as Moss left the room, ending his short stint as a reporter.

1,000th CATCH

It was all set up for Cris Carter, a player who loved the spotlight.

On Nov. 30, 2000, Carter came into a special Thursday night game at the Metrodome against Detroit, in a contest that was nationally televised, needing just four catches to reach the 1,000-catch milestone in his career. He'd join Jerry Rice, widely considered the best receiver ever to play, as the only receivers to reach the feat.

With the bright lights shining on Carter and the country watching, Carter didn't disappoint. He joined the immortal Rice in style.

Cris Carter: The Hall of Fame receiver has perhaps the best pair of hands ever to catch an NFL pass. He went as far as waxing his hands to keep them in great shape. (Photo by Rick A. Kolodziej)

In the second quarter, from the Lions' four-yard line, quarterback Daunte Culpepper dropped back and heaved a floater to the far right corner of the south end zone. Carter, fighting double coverage, leapt and brought down the ball for a touchdown and his 1,000th catch.

It was classic Carter. He leapt, he scored and he made history.

GREATEST MOMENT

When Carter made his 1,000th catch, the Vikings had the game stopped. His family came on the field and there was a short ceremony.

More than a year later, reflecting on his 12 years with the Vikings and playing at the Metrodome, Carter was asked after his final home game as a Viking about his fondest memory at the dome. Carter smiled and didn't hesitate.

It was in the moments after his catch. Carter was showered with hugs and congratulations. Then his eight-year-old daughter, Monterae, sashayed up to her father and whispered something to him.

Carter thought his daughter, dressed in a new dress for the occasion, was going to offer congratulations.

"No," he said, laughing. "There we were in middle of this great moment and she said, 'Daddy, how do you like my hair? I just got it done.' That was great."

STAYING IN SHAPE

Two days after the Vikings won at Dallas on Thanksgiving Day, 2000, star receiver Cris Carter turned 35. Carter, though, was playing like he was 25. He was on his way to another Pro Bowl season and was still dominant,

He was at an age where most players have been retired for a few years. But Carter was feeling great.

"Really, I'm surprised how good I feel," he said. "I feel better than I did when I was 30 or even 25. I don't hurt after games like I did back then."

It certainly wasn't a coincidence that Carter was still performing at a high level at an advanced football age. He watched what he ate, indulging in red meat (a favorite of his) only on special occasions. Plus, he participated in his famous speed camp in Boca Raton, Florida, every off season.

"Age isn't important," he said. "Staying in condition is important. I may be 35, but it's a young 35."

THE HANDS

When one thinks of Cris Carter, it's the hands that come to mind.

Perhaps no receiver in the history of the game had the hands that Cris Carter possessed. Week after week, Carter amazed the NFL with those big, strong, reliable, magical hands.

Many of Carter's 1,100-plus-career catches were made because of those hands. It was as if they had glue all over them.

Carter respected and appreciated his hands as much as anyone. So, of course, he took great care of them. He laughs at how dainty it seems, but Carter treated his hands as if they were diamonds. He had them specially treated weekly.

"I wax and treat them very special," Carter said. "My hands are everything to me."

THE BUSINESS MAN

Tuesdays are the most anticipated day of the season for the NFL. It's the players' one day off during a hectic week.

Most players lounge at home or hit the golf course. The most they usually do is put on a collared shirt and perhaps go to dinner with the family.

But Cris Carter moonlighted on many of his days off. Whether it was flying to Miami, Atlanta or Detroit or doing business in the Twin Cities, Carter was often on the go during the season, working on building Carter Bros. L.L.C., an Atlanta-based construction management company he runs with his brother John.

Armed with a cell phone, fax machine and email, Carter keeps daily tabs of his ventures at his place of football business. His locker stall at Winter Park often turns into a portable desk, holding Carter's uniform, shoes, playbooks and business supplies.

"I have an opportunity in the business world that I can succeed in for the rest of my life," Carter said. "Business is a lot like football for me," he said. "You have to work to succeed; only the well-prepared and talented succeed. Just because I'm a great football player, though, doesn't mean I will be a great businessman. That's why I'm working so hard on it now. I have to be ready."

IT WAS MY LIFE

When Cris Carter's days with the Vikings came to an end, he found himself reflecting on a bigger entity than football—his life. It was in Minnesota where Carter got control of his life. Really, it's in Minnesota where his life was saved.

With his career on the ropes because of addictions to drugs and alcohol, Carter came to Minnesota from Philadelphia. If he didn't shape up in Minnesota, his career would likely have been over.

"But it was more than football, it was my life," Carter said. "I needed to get my life under control. I was an addict.

"This is where I got my life together," Carter said. "Minnesota will always be special to me. I wouldn't be anything if I never came to Minnesota."

Chapter 6

Contemporary Players

BRYANT McKINNIE

Teammates didn't let Bryant McKinnie off easy when he reported to the team eight weeks into the season after a lengthy contract holdout. Older teammates had some good-natured fun with him when he finally joined them. During pre-practice stretching, the veterans had McKinnie sing the University of Miami fight song.

After McKinnie conducted a television interview, tight end Byron Chamberlain couldn't help but have some additional fun with McKinnie.

Chamberlain announced to the entire locker room, "Hey, Bryant was asked what's the difference between playing in college and for the NFL. Bryant said he was paid in cash at Miami and by check in the NFL."

Bryant McKinnie: The Vikings' first-round draft pick in the 2002 draft posed a challenge for the team's equipment managers—finding a uniform big enough to handle his six-foot-eight frame and size 18 feet. (Photo courtesy AP/WWP)

BIG MAN

The addition of Bryant McKinnie was a massive challenge for the team's equipment managers. They had to find something for McKinnie to wear. While finding uniforms that fit huge NFL players is their job, dressing the six-foot-eight, 353-pound McKinnie is a tall, big order.

Nearly every piece of McKinnie's uniform had to be special-ordered. He has size 18 shoes—the biggest longtime equipment manager Dennis Ryan had ever seen. His helmet size, 8 5/8, is the biggest in the NFL. His gloves needed to be special-ordered, and his jersey had to be sewn together because of his unusual length.

"I'd never seen anything like it," Ryan said. "He is not the norm."

HE WAS SPECIAL

Bryant McKinnie's talent level was staggering for his teammates to comprehend. The left tackle, the No. 7 overall choice in the 2002 draft, didn't take long to show his talent level.

He had unusually fast feet for a man his size and was incredibly strong.

"From the first day, you knew he was special," said left guard Corbin Lacina, who played next to McKinnie. "The kid is just something special. He's going to have a long, long career."

GREG BIEKERT

Toward the end of each season, Greg Biekert usually looks back on the year and points to a couple of games where he felt he failed himself and his teammates.

Biekert wasn't scolding himself, though.

"It's unusual, but there aren't any games I wish I had back this year," the Vikings middle linebacker and sudden leader said of his first year with the team. "I think I've played at a high level every game. I don't know if this is my best season ever, but it's up there and that is very satisfying, particularly under the circumstances."

According to the Vikings' defensive statistics for 2002, Biekert had 142 tackles, four shy of his career high. Biekert has flourished since signing with the Vikings. Prior to signing, he was released by Oakland, who thought he had slowed down, for refusing to take a pay cut.

But he has played at a high level since joining the Vikings, who had an interest in Biekert since rumors floated out of Oakland a week before he was released. The Vikings signed him less than 24 hours after he was officially released.

The Vikings needed stability, and defensive coordinator Willie Shaw, who had coached Biekert in Oakland, knew he'd be the perfect leader. The marriage has worked out well.

"I wouldn't want to think about our defense without Biekert," Vikings coach Mike Tice said. "He's been a constant all season."

Biekert said playing with so many young teammates has reenergized him.

"I feel younger being with these guys," Biekert said. "I'm not even as sore as I used to be because these guys are keeping me young ... I love being in this situation and working with these young players and watching them grow. They've helped me stay reenergized as much as I've helped them."

SUPERSTITIONS

Corbin Lacina and Matt Birk have a training camp tradition. It shows camaraderie and dedication, but it is not for the faint of heart.

The two players wear the same clothes every day. While practice is a big part of training camp, the players are in their own street clothes, of course, for much of the day. For Birk and Lacina, packing for camp is not a big chore. Laundry detergent is not necessary.

Each day, the two players are adorned in the same outfit, both wearing a gray t-shirt and dark shorts.

"I've done it since I came in the league in 1993," Lacina said. "It's good luck. I'll always do it."

Lacina talked Birk, his training camp roommate, into joining in the one-outfit look.

"It's great," Birk said. "I don't have to stay up at night, wondering what I'm going to wear the next day."

HOMETOWN BOYS

When Matt Birk was a youngster in St. Paul, he looked up to Corbin Lacina. Birk would go see Lacina play football at Cretin-Derham Hall, a St. Paul high school powerhouse. Birk aspired to be like Lacina—who blocked for eventual Heisman Trophy winner and Carolina Panthers quarterback Chris Weinke—when he got to high school.

Not only did Birk, six years Lacina's junior, become a Raider like Lacina, but he became his teammate, friend, roommate and business partner.

In 1999, a year after Birk was drafted by the hometown Vikings, Lacina joined the team as a free agent after playing

Matt Birk: The Pro Bowl center is the pride of the Twin Cities—a lifelong resident of St. Paul and a former star for Cretin-Derham Hall High. (Photo by Rick A. Kolodziej)

in Buffalo and Carolina. The two quickly became close. They now co-own a gym in St. Paul. They are also roommates in training camp and on the road.

"It's great to get to know Corbin and play next to him," Birk said. "I would have never imagined playing with him when I was 11."

STAYING HOME

Matt Birk just wanted to play in the NFL. He wasn't thinking about ever donning the purple.

Sure, he was a Vikings fan and occasionally attended games as he grew up near downtown St. Paul. But he never imagined playing professional football. Actually, Birk never really thought much about playing college football. When he started to talk about going to Harvard it was for their prestigious economic program alone. Football was just an extra.

However, after a stellar four-year career at Harvard, Birk became a pro prospect. Still, he never imagined being a Viking.

"Cincinnati, St. Louis, it didn't matter," Birk said. "When I was coming out of college, I was just concentrating on being drafted. I never thought that the Vikings would be a possibility. It was a one in 31 shot."

However, five rounds after the Vikings stunned the league by selecting Randy Moss, they shocked St. Paul by taking the homegrown player.

"Everyone in our family and circle of friends was pretty excited on draft day," Birk said. "To think I was going to play in the NFL and do it for the Vikings made it an unbelievable experience."

GROWING INTO A STAR

Matt Birk sat and watched Pro Bowl center Jeff Christy play for two years while he learned the position. However, Birk improved so much and caught on so well that the team didn't feel compelled to keep Christy when he became a free agent after the 1999 season. Christy, along with Randall McDaniel, was the heart and soul of the offensive line for years, but because of Birk's potential, the team felt comfortable allowing Christy to leave for Tampa Bay.

Birk didn't let them down.

He stepped right into the lineup and immediately became a Pro Bowl player. Amazingly, Birk has been voted into the Pro Bowl all three years he's played. That is the type of pace that makes Hall of Fame voters take notice when a career is over.

"Matt was a star from the time he stepped on the field," said Mike Tice, who was Birk's offensive line coach for two years before becoming the head coach. "He was so smart and athletic. He actually got better every day and he still does. He's a special player."

BYRON CHAMBERLAIN

Byron Chamberlain came to the Vikings as a mostly unknown commodity. But the team knew plenty about him when they signed him as a free agent prior to the 2001 season from Denver. They knew he had great hands, great character and a winning pedigree.

He became one of the few players of the past few seasons to own a Super Bowl ring.

"I bring that experience," Chamberlain said, who quickly became a leader of the Vikings. "Being on a Super Bowl winner gives you knowledge of how to get it done. Plus, I can show the guys my rings and show them what we're all playing for."

Chamberlain also contributed on the field. In his first season as a Viking, he became one of the most dangerous tight ends in the league. He caught 57 passes in 2001, 25 more than in any of his previous six NFL seasons, earning him a Pro Bowl berth.

"I've always emulated Shannon Sharpe, the great tight end backed up in Denver," Chamberlain said. "He taught me how to deal with every aspect of the game, and it's gratifying to do something he's done so many times in his career—make the Pro Bowl."

BC'S LITTLE SOLDIERS

Prior to games at the Metrodome, a familiar sight is a large group of children surrounding one of their own, Byron Chamberlain. The Vikings tight end is the leader of BC's Little Soldiers, an affiliation of the Salvation Army. The group benefits children during each Vikings home game, as Chamberlain entertains several of the kids.

Chamberlain requested to assist the Salvation Army because the group assisted him as a child. Chamberlain, his mother, older brother, and sister once spent two months in a Salvation Army shelter in Dallas.

"I don't know where I'd be without that help," Chamberlain said. "So it's important for me to give back to those kids. I tell them all the time I was them when I was their age."

Chamberlain came up with the name of his group for three reasons. For starters, he liked the "Soldiers" connection to the Salvation Army. Secondly, he wants the kids "to solider and march on through their problems." Finally, while playing in Denver, he and best friend Terrell Davis invented the popular "Mile High Salute" to celebrate touchdowns during the Broncos' Super Bowl run in the late 1990s.

"BC's Little Soldiers just seems like a perfect name," Chamberlain said.

GARY ANDERSON

When Gary Anderson re-signed with the Vikings in September, 2002, it amazed his teammates. Anderson, then 43, became the oldest Viking by nine years and is just five months younger than his coach Mike Tice.

Several of the Vikings rookies were astonished to be in the locker room with someone nearly twice their age.

"Guys ask me a lot of questions about what it was like in the old days," Anderson said. "One rookie said I was in the NFL before he was born ... that stuff is pretty funny and scary, too."

Even some of Anderson's older teammates can't comprehend playing with Anderson. They watched him in their youth. He's a walking NFL historian.

"I grew up a big Pittsburgh Steelers fan," linebacker Jim Nelson said. "Gary was on those teams. It's just hard to believe I'm playing with an old Steeler."

OLD FRIENDS

One of Red McCombs's favorite players in his tenure as owner of the Vikings was venerable kicker Gary Anderson.

McCombs joked that he liked Anderson so much because they were close in age.

But McCombs really admired Anderson for his class, professionalism and ability to keep his game at a high level for so many years. It was his admiration for Anderson that made McCombs press for Anderson to return early in the season in 2002.

When Anderson—whose legitimate range was 46-48 yards—nailed a 53-yarder to beat Miami in December, 2002, McCombs was the happiest person in the Vikings' jubilant locker room. He led a raucous cheer for Anderson, who received the game ball.

"Gary is a Hall of Famer and it is a pleasure to be associated with him," McCombs said.

THE FISHERMAN

When he is isn't kicking field goals, Gary Anderson's favorite way to spend a day is fishing. He has been a lifelong fisherman and has tried virtually every type of fishing there is.

"I've fished all over the world," said the South Africa native. "I've deep sea fished in Hawaii and ice fished in Minnesota and pretty much everything in between."

Anderson's favorite type of fishing is fly fishing. In fact, the Vikings had to pry Anderson out of the Colorado River when they re-signed him in September, 2002.

"I was fishing and having the time of my life," Anderson said. "But the phone rang and it was the right team and the right time … I'll have plenty of time to fish but my time to kick in the NFL is more limited. In the meantime, I'll fish in the off season."

RECORD BREAKER

When Gary Anderson broke George Blanda's all-time NFL scoring record—against Buffalo on Oct. 22, 2000— he immediately began thinking of his father.

It seemed the only member of Anderson's family not in attendance at the Metrodome on that special day was his father, Douglas. It was Anderson's father, a soccer player in South Africa, who introduced his son to American football and who was instrumental his college and pro career.

"I wish my father was here," a tearful Anderson said. "I wouldn't even have scored one point in the NFL if it weren't for him ... this is most special day of my life, but if he was here, it would have been even more special."

CARTER HAD NO CONFIDENCE

Gary Anderson didn't realize it at the time—he was a tad busy—but Cris Carter was offering him some motivation when the Vikings beat Carter and the Dolphins on Dec. 21, 2002.

In the afterglow of his 53-yard game-winning field goal that put a crimp in the Dolphins' playoff plans, Anderson overheard Carter on the Dolphins sideline talking about his lack of range.

"CC was walking up and down the sideline saying not to worry, that I couldn't kick it that far," Anderson said with a chuckle.

"He should have known better, that the old guy could still do it. He's no spring chicken, either."

Anderson was right. Carter didn't think Anderson would be able to crank his 43-year-old leg enough to make the 53-yard kick.

"I didn't think he could make it," Carter said.

GLAD WE'RE HERE

Former Dolphins defensive end Lorenzo Bromell said the 2002 victory over Miami was one of the sweetest in his career. He played for Miami for four years before signing with the Vikings this off season.

"I miss my friends over there," Bromell said.

"But I got new friends over here. I'm having a good time."

Defensive end Kenny Mixon and tight end Hunter Goodwin joined Bromell in Minnesota this off season. Mixon, Minnesota's starting left end, had five tackles. Bromell had one. The two shared a sack against their former teammate Jay Fiedler.

A STUDENT OF THE GAME

After an average rookie season in 2001, running back Michael Bennett became a student of the game. He studied film of several of the great running backs of all time.

Ironically, though, one of the most helpful studies for Bennett was watching film of himself—from his successful college days at the University of Wisconsin.

Running backs coach Dean Dalton first noticed Bennett's tendencies in college and pointed them out to

Bennett. In college, Bennett was not tentative and hit the hole, utilizing his great speed.

Bennett came out of his summer film work a different player from his rookie year. Actually, he was the same player he was in college. The result was numerous long runs, more than 1,200 yards rushing, and a spot as Pro Bowl alternate in his second season.

"I feel comfortable again," Bennett said. "Sometimes it just takes looking at what gave you success in the past."

BENNETT SEES STARS

Michael Bennett is a self-described football nut. He studies the history of the game and was a big fan of the great players of all time. He was also partial to the Dallas Cowboys.

Early in his rookie season, former Cowboys stars Troy Aikman and Daryl "Moose" Johnston requested to speak to Bennett as part of their preparation for covering a Vikings game on Fox. Bennett was speechless when a Vikings public relations staffer told him the two former Super Bowl stars wanted to see him.

"They actually wanted me," a wide-eyed Bennett said. "Those guys were my heroes growing up and they wanted to talk to me."

Bennett brought in several items for the two to autograph. "It was an awesome experience," the appreciative Bennett said.

IN HONOR OF JOHNNY U

When Baltimore Colts Hall of Fame quarterback Johnny Unitas suddenly died during the 2002 season, the NFL mourned. As the league held several tributes to the crew-cut kid from Louisville, Vikings running back Michael Bennett held his own poignant tribute.

Bennett showed up to work the day after Unitas's death wearing his Colts blue No. 19 jersey. It was complete with Unitas's name sewn on it. During the workday, when Bennett was wearing his own jersey, he proudly displayed the jersey of the fallen hero in front of his locker on a hanger.

Bennett's grandfather was a big Unitas fan and taught his grandson all about Johnny U. Much to his grandfather's delight, Bennett bought the jersey the summer before Unitas's death.

"He was the greatest," Bennett said of Unitas. "I'm just glad I could learn something about him."

JERSEYS BECOME A TREND

Nary a day would go by in 2002 when a Vikings player wouldn't arrive to work wearing the jersey of another team.

No, the players weren't trying to cause trouble; they were simply paying homage to the stars of the past. Retro jerseys have become very chic, and the tenants of the Vikings' locker room are surely doing their part in making it a trend.

Several players, including tight end Byron Chamberlain, running back Michael Bennett and defensive linemen Chuck Wiley, displayed old-time jerseys. They were not relegated to the NFL, either. The players also wore baseball, NBA and NHL garb.

Michael Bennett: The speedy running back has studied the history of the NFL and often wears the jerseys of his favorite players of old. (Photo by Rick A. Kolodziej)

Among the jerseys Chamberlain—probably the most passionate old-time jersey wearer—would come to work in were 1970s-era Houston Astros, San Diego Padres, Philadelphia 76ers and Buffalo Bill jerseys.

"I'm a big sports fan," Chamberlain said. "I couldn't afford my favorite jerseys when I was a kid, so I'm buying them now and I'm paying tribute to my favorite athletes as well. It's all about the old school."

ROOKIE RITUALS

The rookies always have to do everything. Whether it's carrying the veterans' helmets off the practice field or buying doughnuts for morning meetings, there are certain expectations placed on the youngsters. Hey, it's better than being taped to the goal post, which usually happens to one unlucky rookie each training camp.

In 2001, rookie wide receiver Cedric James was given a unique assignment by his fellow receivers. They had a fantasy football league and made James the commissioner of the league. He had to keep updated statistics and pass out information for his fellow receivers.

James took the job very seriously. He even kept the information in a briefcase and brought it to work every day.

"Everyone has to pay their dues," James said. "This is how I'll pay mine."

CARS THEY DRIVE

The Vikings' players parking lot is a virtual who's who of new luxury cars. Nearly every type of fancy new ride sits in the lot each day. Many players are in tune with the trend amongst athletes of driving huge militaristic Hummers.

But the clear automobile aficionado is quarterback Daunte Culpepper. The man loves his vehicles. Culpepper owns more than five cars and trucks and often brings a different vehicle to work every day.

His pride and joy is a dark green Mercedes.

"That's my baby," Culpepper said. "It's my favorite."

BUSINESS MAN

Robert Tate departed the team in 2002 after five years with the team, but his presence was in the locker room on a daily basis.

Nearly every player on the roster had several pieces of Tate's casual wear. Tate's line of clothes, mostly sweatsuits and sweatshirts, is named "Many Miles Traveled," a tribute to his journey to the NFL.

"I love clothes and I like being a businessman," the cornerback said. "It's great to see all of my teammates wear my clothes every day. It makes me proud."

IT'S GOT TO BE THE SHOES

The Vikings' equipment managers are often the unsung heroes of the team. Not only are they in charge of all of the equipment and making sure the players are comfortable, but they also have to be meteorologists as well.

For each road game, the equipment managers must decide if extra clothing and shoes are necessary, depending on the expected conditions for game day. On Thanksgiving Day, 2000, their Boy Scout-like preparation paid off in spades.

The equipment managers, anticipating rain to pour through the hole in Texas Stadium, brought special turf shoes and extra uniforms for the players just in case. As expected, a steady and hard rainstorm pelted the field in the first half, making running a slip-and-slide adventure. Having trouble with the weather, the Vikings led just 10-9 at halftime.

However, in addition to a talk by coach Dennis Green at halftime, the players went through a quick uniform and shoe change. They got out of their wet clothes and put on shoes that had better traction.

The change did the Vikings wonders. They came out fresh and on steady ground, scoring 17 unanswered points in the third quarter to easily route the drenched Cowboys 27-15.

To show his appreciation, Green gave the equipment team the game ball.

"Those guys came up big for us," Green said. "They were the heroes of that game."

GIVING BACK

Many players gave back to their former schools, but receiver Chris Walsh goes beyond the call of duty.

Each year, Walsh sends hundreds of pairs of game-used shoes to his high school, Ygnacio Valley, in Concord, California. Walsh arranges it with the Vikings' equipment managers to save the shoes after they are done being used.

The high school players then use the shoes in their games. The kids look forward to the arrival of the shoes like their Christmas presents. For the players, many of whom who can't afford high-quality cleats, they are gifts. It's a thrill for them to see the shoes with Daunte Culpepper's No. 11 or Robert Smith's No. 26 written on the back of them.

"Often NFL players use the shoes just once or twice, and I hate to see them go to waste," Walsh said. "The high school players need the shoes, and they are still in great shape. It's a real thrill for these players to wear the same shoe that Randy Moss or Cris Carter once wore. It makes them feel special, and it makes me feel good, too."

ROBERT SMITH

Robert Smith was always known for doing the unexpected and for being unpredictable. But he saved his biggest surprise for last.

In early February 2001, Smith quietly announced his retirement from the NFL at the tender age of 28. He was coming off one of his greatest seasons and he was expected to sign a new five-year contract that would set him up financially for the rest of his life.

But Smith, with varied interests, decided to call it quits.

"Robert is different, and he showed that by retiring when he still had so much time left as a player," Mike Tice said. "I respect him for it. He wanted to move on and he did."

COREY CHAVOUS

Corey Chavous's house is more like a film study room. Why wouldn't it be? After all, Chavous spends more time with film than Ron Howard or Steven Spielberg.

The Vikings' defensive back is renowned for his diligent film work. Chavous not only watches film at Winter Park, but he watches film at home. He watches film during the season, and also dissects it during the off season.

"I'm a major film buff," Chavous said. "I watched film before I even played. I learn so much from it. It keeps me sharp."

That explains why Chavous often has four VCRs taping games during the weekend. He tapes more than 25 hours of football—college and pro—each weekend. He has a video library of about 1,000 tapes of several sports, including football, basketball, baseball and boxing.

"I'm a sports nut," Chavous said. "Find me the biggest Vikings fan and I think I'm just as big of a fan. It just so happens that I'm a player as well as a fan."

THE DRAFTNIK

Vikings defensive back Corey Chavous has been studying the NFL draft since he was seven years old. It is his passion. Call him Mel Kiper in shoulder pads. Unlike most draft gurus, however, Chavous, considered by many scouts to be one of the most intelligent players in the league, can run the 40-yard dash in the same range as the players he studies. What other player in the league shows up at college campuses to watch players work out?

Chavous became interested in sports at age five and became particularly interested in the NFL because his uncle Barney Chavous was in the midst of a 14-year career in the league. His fascination with the draft began in '83 because he loved quarterbacks.

Chavous threw himself into scouting and began taping college games as an elementary school student in Aiken, S.C.

"By the end of the season, I've seen nearly every draftable player at least once," Chavous said. "My studying of the draft is really a yearlong project."

A SPORTS NUT

Corey Chavous can easily blurt out obscure trivia for nearly every sport. His favorite sports figures, though, include Dan Marino, Sam Snead and Boris Becker.

*Corey Chavous: The defensive back studies the NFL draft
like an NFL scout. Many think after his playing days are
over he'll have a future as a talent evaluator.
(Photo courtesy of Elsa/Getty Images)*

"Corey was known as an aspiring Howard Cosell in the neighborhood," said his mother, Te'Verra. "People relied on his sports knowledge. ...He just threw himself into sports. It got to the point where I just gave up trying to have some family time on Saturday and Sunday afternoons. He'd be in front of the TV watching every sporting event he could find."

Chavous said his hobby helped him become a better player. Because he has long charted the strengths and weaknesses of other players, it helped him realize that he too has strengths and weaknesses.

"It's the reality of sports—everyone does some things well and some things poorly," Chavous said. "I got things to work on to be the best cover corner I can be. But I'm OK with it. Like I see on film, it takes work to get better, and I'm willing to do it."

MOVIE STAR

The Hollywood types were looking for a mean actor who could play the role of a nasty character named Satan. The role was for an action movie made by Universal Pictures, entitled *Tara*. The film starred rapper/actor Ice-T.

The producers were looking for an intimidating, hulking man for the Satan role. A friend of a friend mentioned to the producers a pro football player they knew who'd be perfect for the role.

The producers took one look at defensive end Chuck Wiley, who stands six foot four and weighs close to 300 pounds. His hair is long and dredlocked, and his goatee is also long. He looks scary.

"I guess I fit the role," said the truly amiable Wiley. "I don't want people to think I'm Satan-like. It's just a movie. It was a great opportunity. But I'm really a nice guy. Movies are just movies."

DEALING WITH INJURIES

Chris Walsh was long considered one of the Vikings' toughest players. He was a gritty special teams player who used his body with reckless abandon. He'd missile down the field and hurtle his body, all in the name of making a special teams tackle.

But Walsh's reputation as a tough guy went to a different level in 2000 when he suffered a broken jaw and didn't miss a beat.

Walsh suffered the upper jaw break on a helmet-to-helmet hit in St. Louis. With the playoffs a month away, coach Dennis Green was concerned Walsh's season would be in jeopardy because of the injury. After all, Walsh was forced to have surgery two days after the injury, so his availability certainly looked bleak.

But this was Chris Walsh we're talking about. He took one day to recuperate and then bugged Green to get on the practice field. Green incredulously humored his special teams ace and allowed him to practice. But Walsh went on the practice field and performed with no problems.

Equipped with a specially designed helmet, Walsh played the next week and the rest of the season without incident.

"Amazing," Green said. "Not too many players can play with a broken jaw. But Chris is a special kind of tough guy.

FAMILY AFFAIR

Jake Reed always took care of his younger brother, Dale Carter. Reed is two years older than his brother and looked after him as the two grew up in Covington, Georgia.

So when Dale Carter joined the Vikings in 2001, Reed was thrilled. It was the first time the two had played together since high school. Their careers took them on different paths. Reed, a sure-handed receiver, went to Grambling and then went on to enjoy a long career with the Vikings. Carter, one of the most dominant cornerbacks in the NFL in the mid-1990s, played at Tennessee and then played in the NFL with Kansas City and Denver.

Finally, the two were reunited with the Vikings. They took advantage of being together. Reed had Carter live with his family and the two were inseparable at Winter Park.

"I took care of Dale Carter when he was a kid and I'll do it again," Reed said. "We've waited to be together for a long time."

MOE WILLIAMS

Moe Williams passes Bill Brown's tough-guy test.

So Brown was rooting harder than anyone during the 2002 season when Williams broke his record for consecutive games with a rushing touchdown. Williams scored touchdowns in seven straight games, breaking Brown's record of six set in 1968. Brown was at the Metrodome on Nov. 17 to see Williams break the record against Green Bay.

"I don't mind that Moe broke it. Most of the records I set are gone and that's fine," said Brown, who was known for his hard-nosed play with the Vikings from 1962-74. "I know Moe and he's a good kid. I love the way he plays. He's very tough; he gets after it like I did. He's the type of guy I like."

Brown said the record is a tribute to Williams's toughness.

"You have to have in your heart the want to score," Brown said. "That's a lot of determination to pound it into the end zone week after week."

TEAMMATES STAND BEHIND LEWIS KELLY

When tragedy struck Lewis Kelly in the summer of 2002, his offensive linemates knew they would have an added duty.

"We've all talked about it and we're going to do all we can for Lewis," Vikings left guard Corbin Lacina said. "He needs us to be there for him, and we will be. We're going to support him in any way possible."

Kelly's wife Rakiva, 24, died Aug. 25, 2002, of complications from a rare blood disorder. She died two hours after miscarrying her four-month baby. Kelly's offensive linemates, coaches and other Vikings attended a Twin Cities memorial. Kelly told his teammates he would be leaning on them this season.

"He was amazing," center Matt Birk said. "It was like he was there to console everyone else. He had great strength. ... But he also needs us, and we know that."

HANGING IN THERE

The death of his wife was obviously devastating to Lewis Kelly. However, he said being around his teammates helped him survive the utter pain that filled his heart.

Kelly would get to the facility early and leave late. He filled his time by immersing himself in weightlifting and watching film. He also found solace in talking to his teammates and trying to love and enjoy himself.

Anything to keep his mind off his pain.

"I don't know where I'd be without these guys," Kelly said. "I owe them a lot. They're keeping my spirits up."

His teammates and coaches tried their best. Close friends, tight end Byron Chamberlain and his wife Inga, spent a lot of time with him, and several teammates also extended dinner invitations. Coach Mike Tice and his family had Kelly over to their house several times for dinner.

"We're all here for him," said offensive linemate Chris Liwienski. "This is a devastation and we all want to pull Lewis out of this."

WIILIE HOWARD, THE BIG BROTHER

Vikings defensive lineman Willie Howard became a father during the 2002 season. Many players have children, but Howard's foray into parenthood was a tad different. Howard, at age 24, gained full legal guardianship of his 14-year-old sister, Crystal.

His sister moved to the Twin Cities after spending eight years in foster care in Northern California. Howard has kept in constant contact with his sister.

At Stanford, he occasionally would be excused from practice so he could make the three-hour drive to visit his sister. He promised her that when he had the means, he would petition to become her guardian. Howard's mother, stepfather and 15-year-old brother all moved to Eden Prairie from the Bay Area after Howard was drafted. Finally. Howard had his family together.

"It's finally happening," he said. "I couldn't be happier. I will be a parent figure, but I will still be her big brother. It's the most important thing I've done."

LIFE ON THE PRACTICE SQUAD

There are 58 men in the Vikings locker room, but only 53 dress for games. Yet the five young players who compose the Vikings practice squad every year are very much a part of the team.

The practice squad players spend all week preparing the veteran players for the games. They practice, go to meetings, and work out with the team. They just don't play on Sundays. It's not perfect, but for a young player who still needs seasoning, it's a great opportunity.

"There are no promises when you are on the practice squad," said tight end Matt Cercone, who shuttled back and forth from the practice squad three times in two years. "But it is still football, and it's still a chance."

In addition to being in the least secure position in the locker room—most of them live in hotels because it makes no sense for them to sign a lease—the practice squad players are the lowest-paid, earning $4,000 a week. Because of the extra week this season, they will be paid for 18 weeks. If the Vikings make the playoffs, they will be awarded an additional $4,000 a week, so a player on the practice squad all season would make $72,000. The lowest-paid players on the 53-man roster are first-year players making the NFL minimum of $209,000.

"You dress right next to a millionaire, and then you're not making that much," said cornerback Don Morgan, who was on the active roster after spending parts of the past two seasons on the practice squad. "It's motivational. It's like you're really not in the NFL. You're close, but you're not there yet."

REMEMBERING THEIR BEGINNING

Several veterans started their career on the practice squad. They don't forget their humble start.

"The guys always talk to me about it, and I'm here for them," said tight end Byron Chamberlain, who spent 11 weeks on Denver's practice squad in 1995. "It's a tough road. You question yourself a lot, so there are guys around to help show you the way."

Offensive tackle Chris Liwienski said he thinks about his days as a practice squad player daily.

"You have to chase your dream, and being on the practice squad is a part of it for a lot of guys in the NFL," Liwienski said. "It just makes you hungry because you're almost there, but you're not there yet. Once I was on the practice squad, I wanted more."

JOHN RANDLE

To say John Randle captured the imagination of opposing offenses would be an extreme understatement. All eyes were always on Randle, widely considered one of the most dominant inside pass rushers in NFL history.

To Randle's defensive teammates, the concentration on him was astonishing. They could see the offensive players shift and adjust because of Randle on every play.

"It was amazing to watch," linebacker Kailee Wong said. "You should see what they did to him. Teams put two, three guys on him every play ... The play just collapses on John. Every play, he has to deal with that."

He couldn't be covered with just a guard, as most players at his position require.

Instead, Randle got some combination of multiple coverages. Whether it was two guards, a guard, center and the halfback or two guards and the center, the one constant was that Randle received the heart of team's coverages.

Because he took so much heat, his coaches and teammates called him a hero, the ultimate personal sacrificer.

"He's made a big difference on this defense just by being there," Vikings defensive coordinator Emmitt Thomas said. "The linebackers were better because of Johnny, the defensive backs were better because of Johnny and the other defensive linemen were better because of Johnny."

UNDRAFTED SUCCESS

John Randle was a rarity. No, it has nothing to do with the facial war paint or his never-ending energy even though it was always impressive to see him have that game-day speed in an April minicamp.

But what made Randle truly special was the road he took to become an NFL star and a future NFL Hall of Famer. Randle joined the Vikings in 1990 as an undrafted free agent.

Most players who come into the NFL without being drafted leave it quickly. What Randle did was leave his mark. He quickly emerged as a special talent and became a perennial Pro Bowl player. In retrospect, Randle said his journey was his biggest source of pride.

"Nothing came easy for me," Randle said.

"But I wouldn't have it any other way. I took nothing for granted. I needed to prove myself to make it and I never stopped trying to prove myself. Not being drafted instilled a special work ethic in me."

John Randle: The veteran defensive tackle was a
self-made star. With his motor always going, Randle
even practiced his trade while grocery shopping.
(Photo by Rick A. Kolodziej)

ALWAYS ON THE JOB

One day in the early 1990s, longtime Vikings coach and personnel director Paul Wiggin saw a young John Randle in a grocery store, doing his shopping. Randle didn't see his coach.

Wiggin stood there amazed and amused, watching the energetic Randle shop. Wiggin already knew Randle was an intense player who does everything at full speed. Throughout his career, Randle always sprinted to each different drill during practice while the majority of his teammates would jog from station to station.

Wiggin's jaw dropped, however, when he saw Randle treat the supermarket like the practice field. Randle was racing around the store, picking up his items. When he came across a large display, Randle would treat it like it was a gigantic left tackle and try to get by it.

"Here's Johnny, doing the swim move [a popular move by defensive ends] against a pile of potato chips," Wiggin said. "I couldn't believe what I was seeing. Johnny was playing football in the grocery store. I knew we had something special then. While other guys were playing golf on their off days, Johnny was battling a bag of potato chips."

TEDDY, VIKING FOR A DAY

While Randle was known for his intensity, he also had a lighter side. In fact, he was one of the most humorous players on the team.

During the 2000 season, he showed his spontaneity and sense of humor. At Winter Park, players and employees often get several things in the mail to be autographed. One day, an employee got a teddy bear in the mail. The idea is to write a diary for the bear and then send the stuffed animal on to another friend. Basically, it's a chain letter.

Well, Randle got hold of the bear and had a field day. He essentially made the unsuspecting bear a member of the team. He had it photographed with several players, brought in the cafeteria and even had its furry ankles taped on the training table as if it were going to practice that day.

He photographed everything and then sent it on its way to its surprised owner.

RELIEVING HIMSELF ON FIELD

Randle liked to have fun on the field. He was, in his own words, "wild" and would celebrate after a big play or a big sack. The bigger the game, the bigger the celebration.

However, in the 2000 playoffs, in a divisional round victory over New Orleans at the Metrodome that sent the Vikings to the NFC championship game for the second time in three seasons, Randle got a little carried away.

After sacking Saints quarterback Aaron Brooks, Randlle got on all fours and crawled across the field and lifted his leg, simulating a dog relieving himself.

It was hilarious—if not tasteless—and the entire Metrodome roared in laughter.

However, the NFL didn't find it funny. Randle was fined $7,500 for his excessive celebration.

RANDLE-FAVRE

Who could ever forget a rabid-eyed John Randle chasing around that rooster in a television commercial in the mid-1990s? Making the commercial both clever and hilarious, the rooster was scrambling around the pen wearing a tiny, snug Green Bay Packers No. 4 jersey.

There was Randle—as intense as he is on the field and complete with his patented war paint on his face—feverishly running after the rooster. The message, of course, was that Randle was doing everything he could to prepare to conquer Green Bay quarterback Brett Favre, his NFC Central rival.

The premise was very real. Randle and Favre became intense rivals. Whenever the Vikings and Packers played, these two (the best players on their respective units) would do battle.

"I've always loved playing against Johnny Randle," Favre said. "He's a battler who comes after me every time we play."

DAUNTE CULPEPPER

When Daunte Culpepper burst on the NFL scene in 2000, his offensive coordinator was used to the beginner's luck. Sherman Lewis was also Brett Favre's offensive coordinator in his first year as a starter in Green Bay, eight years earlier.

"I found myself thinking about those days a lot and remembering how I dealt with Brett back then," Lewis said. "Those days have certainly helped me deal with Daunte. I think about working with a young quarterback and what I did to help things and what Brett needed. I try to think back as much as I can. It's a similar situation."

Like Favre, Culpepper enjoyed early success in Lewis's offense. Culpepper said he felt comfortable learning the NFL under the man who guided Favre in his own infant stages.

"Coach Sherm has been very good with me," Culpepper said. "He has helped a lot with his experience and his ideas. He gives me advice a lot."

Lewis said both players were similar in their approach in their early days as the signal caller.

"They're both very aggressive and confident in themselves," he said. "A young Brett thought he could do it all, and Daunte believes in himself, too. They're both easy to work with."

Daunte Culpepper was often compared to another Vikings star quarterback, Fran Tarkenton, because like his predecessor, Culpepper can run all day. But those who know say there's really no comparison.

"Culpepper is much faster than Tarkenton ever was," said former Vikings coach Jerry Burns, who was the offensive coordinator when Tarkenton was the Vikings' quarterback. "Really, Culpepper is the fastest quarterback I've seen. There's been no one with that much speed. At his size, he can really take off and hurt people. Tarkenton ran for a different reason. He ran back and forth to find time for his receivers to get open. ... Culpepper is much more dangerous."

Because Culpepper is a hulking six foot four, 260 pounds, Burns said his ability to run over opponents makes him more dangerous than the smaller, sleeker Tarkenton, who succeeded by wearing down bigger defenders by scrambling for what seemed to be minutes at a time.

"He'll always be a running threat," Burns said. "He'll come right at you....He could be the best running quarterback ever because of his size and speed.

"Culpepper is definitely different. The Vikings have never seen anything like him before."

HONORING THY MOTHER

Daunte Culpepper ran out of the Vikings' locker room in New Orleans with his tie barely around his neck. The Vikings had just won their first road game in more than two years and a party atmosphere was ensuing.

But Culpepper was trying his best to get out of the locker room. He was trying to see his adoptive mother, Emma Culpepper.

Culpepper was one of several children Emma Culpepper took into her foster care over the years. She was drawn to the young Daunte and ended up adopting him. The two were extremely close. He once said his favorite childhood memory was staying home and hanging out with his mother.

Because she lived in Orlando, in a custom home he built for her, his mother didn't get to see him often. She would occasionally go to games in the South. In New Orleans, she made it to one of his best games of the season. He scored two touchdowns running, threw for two more and won the game on a two-point play on a run with five seconds remaining.

He gave her four of the scoring game balls.

"She's my hero," Culpepper said. "If it wasn't for her, I wouldn't be doing this or anything, really."

HI MOM

Ed McDaniel had a simple tradition that touched his heart nearly every day. After every interview during his career in front of television cameras, McDaniel would looked into the camera, wave his hand and say "Hi Mom." No matter if the interview was nationally televised—where his mother could possibly see it from her South Carolina home—or if it was simply a local Twin Cities station, which his mother had no chance of seeing, McDaniel finished each interview the same way.

The simple but thoughtful message of love was a popular trend in the league in the 1980s. Cameras would catch McDaniel on the bench after a big play and on cue he'd smile, wave and say hello to his mother.

McDaniel took notice of the league-wide gestures of motherly love while he was in high school and in college while playing at Clemson. He decided that was the message of thanks, he wanted to pass to his mother. So for his entire career, McDaniel always gave a "Hi Mom."

"It's my thing," McDaniel. "It's my special thing to do."

WINNING THE GAME FOR MOM

The day before the Vikings' game against Detroit on Oct. 13, 2002, defensive back Corey Chavous called his family's South Carolina home as he always does. He was given some disturbing news.

His mother Te'Verra was taken to the emergency room that week because she became ill. She ended up being fine, and his family told Chavous they didn't want to worry him about it. But, of course, it weighed on his mind.

So, instead of worrying about it, Chavous decided to put his anxiety to work in his favor. Boy, did it pay off for the Vikings, who entered the game against the Lions staggering with a 0-4 record. The next day, on the final play of the game, Chavous saved the game and gave Mike Tice his first NFL victory by intercepting a pass in the end zone that would have given Detroit a last-second victory.

Chavous left the Metrodome both a hero and a thoughtful son. He took home the ball he intercepted and sent it home to his mother.

"She didn't have a good week," Chavous said. "But maybe this will make her feel better."

'TIS THE SEASON

Daunte Culpepper didn't get Christmas presents as a child. He had a difficult upbringing, and when Emma Culpepper adopted him, the goal of the household was simply to create a loving envrionment and to feed the several children under the guardianship of the elderly woman. Material things such as Christmas presents just weren't a reality of his childhood.

However, when Culpepper became a Viking, he made it a priority to help other kids in his situation to have a chance to enjoy Christmas. So he organized an annual Christmas party for the African-American adoption agency.

The large party is held in the team's indoor practice facility and several teammates attend.

And the kids receive gifts.

"It really warms my heart to bring some Christmas joy to these kids," Culpepper said. "I know what they've gone through and I want to make some good Christmas memories for them."

BORN TO ELF

Perhaps it was because they were rookies. You know, all the embarrassing jobs go to the rookies. Or maybe it was just because they fit the suits.

But it really wasn't a surprise to see rotund offensive lineman Ed Ta'amu play Santa Claus and diminutive wide receivers Kelly Campbell and Nick Davis play his two elves at the Vikings' team Christmas party in 2002.

Each rookie roamed around playing his part, easily at terms with their tasks and happily prancing around in their colorful outfits, spreading Christmas cheer to their amused teammates and their families.

"You should have seen it," said one partygoer. "Those guys were hilarious. Kelly Campbell was born to be an elf."

CHRIS HOVAN

Vikings defensive tackle Chris Hovan is known for his intensity. He always has his game face on. So it's no surprise that Hovan spent the 80-minute drive from the Twin Cities to his first training camp in Mankato preparing himself mentally for his newest challenge.

"As soon as I got in the car I became all business," said the rookie defensive lineman after his first NFL training camp practice Tuesday. "I turned off the radio. I wanted silence. I just wanted to think. It was an hour and 20 minutes of think time. I was preparing for my new life.

"I said 'Chris, this is it. This is what you wanted. Forget about the other pleasures in life. It's all football now.' I have to fully concentrate on this team, and that's exactly what I wanted to do."

NOT WELCOME IN WISCONSIN

You won't see Chris Hovan strolling the streets of Green Bay or even Milwaukee or Madison for that matter. In the

*Chris Hovan: The energetic defensive tackle certainly doesn't
have a fan club in Wisconsin. The intense Hovan has established
a heated rivalry with Green Bay icon Brett Favre.
(Photo by Rick A. Kolodziej)*

long, storied rivalry between the Vikings and Packers, the
energetic defensive tackle has his own category.

During the 2002 season, Hovan became a key figure in
the rivalry. First, in a game at the Metrodome, Hovan went
helmet to helmet in several heated discussions with the Packers' equally fiery quarterback, Brett Favre. Before the second game in Green Bay, Hovan said he was going after Favre,
calling him "the prize."

That had Green Bay fans,who are very protective of their
team and beloved quarterback, on high alert. The fans were
on Hovan hard during the game at Lambeau Field, which
ended in a wild melee on the field. Hovan was bombarded

with debris from the stands as he went to the Vikings' locker room.

He then added words that will forever be etched in the juicy history of this rivalry: "They spit on me and threw garbage at me," Hovan said. "Those Wisconsin people are all class."

And, boy, is the rivalry on.

WRESTLING STARS?

Chris Hovan and tight end Jim Kleinsasser both have that wrestling edge to them. The pair sport wild hairdos and are quite muscular.

"We like the wrestling look and the edge that goes with it," Hovan said. "We sit in my basement and watch it all the time."

So it's no surprise the two became close with Minnesota native and pro wrestling star Brock Lesner, better known on the mat as The Next Big Thing. Hovan and Kleinsasser went to see Lesner—er, Big Thing—wrestle several times and the three even worked out together.

Hovan said he got a taste of the wrestling persona the night in Green Bay when fans threw garbage at him when he left the field.

"It was fun," Hovan said. "I've watched WWF all my life and I felt like the villain entering the ring that night. Now I know how all those guys feel. It was cool."

HIGH SCHOOL BUDDIES

The 2002 Vikings certainly weren't the best team in the NFL, but they led the league in high school connections.

Remarkably, the Vikings had five pairs of players who attended the same high school. Nearly 20 percent of the roster went to the same high school. And that's not even counting the fact that brothers Mike and John Tice were coached at Central Islip High School on Long Island, New York.

The Vikings' high school reunion members were center Matt Birk and Corbin Lacina (St. Paul's Cretin-Derham), defensive back Tyrone Carter and linebacker Henri Crockett (Pompano Beach, Florida's Ely High), long snapper Brody Liddiard and kicker Hayden Epstein (San Diego's Torrey Pines), defensive back Corey Chavous and receiver D'Wayne Bates (Aiken, South Carolina's Silver Bluff) and quarterback Daunte Culpepper and his cousin, receiver Kenny Clark (Ocala, Florida's Vanguard).

All the pairs but Birk and Lacina went to school together. "It's amazing to think I'm in the pros with someone from high school," Chavous said. "It's unusual to say the least."

FOR THE DOGS

If for some reason one missed the outcome of the Vikings game the day before, all they'd have to do to find out if they won was to look for Hudson Steussie. He was the yellow lab owned by Vikings offensive lineman Todd Steussie.

If the scrappy Hudson was on the Vikings' premises, it meant the Vikings were celebrating a victory from the day before. Everyone was in a great mood on the day after a game. Pizza flowed in the locker room, coaches were more visible in the locker room, Steussie's dog would run free.

Hudson would happily feast on some of the thousands of shoes that were in players' lockers. Steussie and his teammates would play fetch with him using a roll of tape.

"He's a good luck charm for us," Steussie said. "He loves coming out here and hanging with the guys."

Randy Moss also enjoys bringing his dogs out to Winter Park. He'd occasionally bring a pair of small, terrier-type dogs to roam the vast practice fields after workouts. Moss and some teammates would jog and play with the dogs.

In typical sassy fashion, Moss played coy when asked what type of dogs they were.

"They're called none-of-your-business dogs," he said.

ROBERT GRIFFITH

When he isn't jarring balls loose by plowing into receivers, Robert Griffith is shining his cheekbones and learning his lines.

In addition to being a standout defensive back, Griffith was a model and actor. He appeared in several magazines and appeared in a music video by R&B singer Kelly Price, starring as the boyfriend of actress Vivica Fox. Griffith plans to become a full-time actor after his playing days.

"I love the lifestyle," Griffith said. "I love entertainment and getting to know all the actors and actresses. When I'm done in this field, I want to excel in Hollywood."

His moonlighting wasn't lost on his teammates.

"Griff is a pretty boy," punter and friend Mitch Berger said. "He's Mr. Hollywood."

JIM KLEINSASSER

Tight end Jim Kleinsasser is definitely a new breed of NFL player.

You often hear the old-timers talk about today's players being bigger, faster and stronger than they were in their days. Well, they're talking about Jim Kleinsasser. The rugged North Dakota native is a massive man at six foot three, 280 pounds. That's a decent size for an offensive or defensive lineman, but mammoth for a tight end.

"I was shocked when I saw Jimmy for the first time," Vikings running back Michael Bennett said. "I love running behind him. Running behind Jimmy is like having a big 18-wheeler in front of you."

Kleinsasser's unique size helps make him a devastating blocker.

"That kid can block like no other tight end I've seen," said Vikings personnel head Paul Wiggin, a former defensive lineman in the 1960s. "He can simply blow humans up. That size of his is amazing."

TALES FROM 9-11-2001

When the world stopped, the Vikings had the day off. It was Tuesday morning, and the Vikings were trying to regroup from a stunning season-opening defeat at home to Carolina. They spent the day before trying to correct the problems and preparing for a Monday night football game at Baltimore.

Then everything changed.

Several players were lifting weights at Winter Park when news reports broke about the terrorist attack on the country. Like every other American, the Vikings players—still trying to get over the shocking death of teammate and friend Korey Stringer—were deeply saddened and worried about the safety of their friends and family who were near the areas that were under attack.

Players Cris Carter, Matt Birk and Kailee Wong were among those who had friends working at or near the World Trade Center. Owner Red McCombs also had a friend working in the World Trade Center. All of their friends, however, were found safe.

Rookie linebacker Fearon Wright's family lived in New York, and his mother used the subway station underneath the World Trade Center every day on her way to work. It took Wright a day to make sure his family was safe.

"This affected everyone," coach Dennis Green said. "We all felt this tragedy."

THE DAY AFTER

Wednesday, Sept. 12, 2001, the Vikings reluctantly returned to Winter Park to prepare for their Monday night football game at Baltimore against former offensive coordinator Brian Billick and the world champion Ravens.

However, no one had their heart in it. Like most players, the Vikings players didn't want to play that weekend.

The initial shock of the horrific event was still very much on their minds, and New York City was still on red alert. The World Trade Center was on fire, and the search for survivors was frantically under way.

Playing a game that weekend just didn't seem right. Defensive backs Robert Griffith and Robert Tate, the team's union representatives, spent two nights on a teleconference call with other team reps to discuss whether to play or not.

On Thursday, the league, at the players' urging, decided to take the weekend off and push back the regular season one week.

"It was the right decision," Griffith said. "We were all affected, but hearing the stories from the players in New York was stunning. The Giants players could see the smoke from their facility and the Meadowlands parking lot was being used as a rescue station. It was no time for football. The right decision was made."

A LASTING EFFECT

For the rest of the 2001 season, the terrible events of Sept. 11 and the tragic effect it had on the country took its toll on the Vikings.

Players said they often thought of the tragedy during the season. Many said the national anthem had a different meaning for them after the events of Sept. 11.

Obviously, players always appreciated the national anthem and used it as a time to make final mental preparations before kickoffs. However, the national anthem took on a more poignant meaning after Sept. 11. Many players reflected about the events and American pride during the anthem.

"I get tears in my eyes during the anthem now," offensive lineman Corbin Lacina said. "Sept. 11 changed everything and it definitely changed the way I get ready for games during the national anthem. It's really amazing."

THE FLYOVER

It was a moment where verbal communication wasn't necessary.

It was just a nod. Perhaps life was getting back to normal a little bit. On Friday, Sept. 14, 2001, the United States was trying to pick up the pieces, three days after the terrorists stunned and crippled the country.

The Vikings were holding a light practice outside, the day after the NFL cancelled the upcoming weekend's games. The practice was solemn, but they were trying to get back to normal.

The airlines were also trying to get some normalcy. The government decided to lift the three-day air ban and began to allow commercial airlines to start flying the skies on a limited schedule that day.

Suddenly, a plane flew over the team's practice field. Since Winter Park is less than 10 miles from the Minneapolis-St. Paul International airport, flyovers are common.

However, this day, the sight was stunning and welcome.

As the lone plane glided through the sky, several players and onlookers looked up. Finally, some normalcy. Running back Doug Chapman, waiting in line for a blocking exercise, looked up, smiled and nodded to teammates.

Chapter 7

Mike Tice

THE SPRINTER

On the first morning of Tice's first training camp practice, he wanted to make sure his team was physically prepared for the season. So he had each player run 14 consecutive wind sprints.

To help team morale, Tice ran the sprints with the players.

"I couldn't believe it," tight end Byron Chamberlain said. "You don't see coaches run like that. He was out there with us, like one of the guys."

It wasn't easy, but the lumbering Tice—who had a few practice runs in the early summer—finished the 14 sprints. But not before he pulled a hamstring on the 13th sprint. Tice had a souvenir (a bruise the size of a New York strip) on the back of his upper leg for the duration of camp.

"Coach is tough," linebacker Henri Crockett said. "He got hurt but finished the job. It was inspiration for us."

THE JINX IS ON

Mike Tice is admittedly a superstitious person. He believes in jinxes. He doesn't like pressing his luck.

So when he began his first season as the Vikings head coach with an 0-4 record, he was scrutinizing everything, including what his wife Diane kept in their refrigerator.

Unbeknownst to the coach, Diane Tice had a bottle of champagne chilling in the refrigerator before the season. She brought the bottle to Champaign, Illinois for the season opener against Chicago and to the Metrodome against Buffalo. The Vikings lost both games, so she didn't bring the bottle to another game.

But when the Vikings beat Detroit in their fifth game to give Tice his first win, the bubbly was uncorked. A victory cigar accompanied the champagne.

"Now we can celebrate—a little," Tice said, a cigar aficionado.

Diane Tice wasn't the only coach's wife to prepare a celebration. Donna Dalton, wife of running backs coach Dean Dalton, made a cake with an inscription, marking Tice's first win.

"Once we started losing, we scraped off the words and gave it to our kids to bring to school for lunch," Dalton said.

NO WEIGHT WATCHER

Mike Tice's first year as the Vikings coach wasn't easy on his waistline.

As the Vikings losses piled up, so did Tice's weight. Asked at the end of the season what was the worst part of his 6-10 maiden voyage, Tice didn't hesitate.

"I didn't like gaining 26 pounds," he said. "We lost and I ate."

Still, Tice, six foot eight, who played at 280 pounds, quickly slimmed back down in the off season.

"Hopefully, winning will keep me fairly skinny," he said.

MR. TMI

Mike Tice would often tell a joke and then stop himself and say "TMI."

"My wife always says TMI around me," he said with a laugh. "Too much information. She says I give too much information."

He sure does. A prankster and always one to make people laugh, one of Tice's favorite jokes is to talk about his hemorrhoids. TMI, indeed.

During a game in his first season, television cameras caught him telling linebackers coach Brian Baker after a particularly poor play: "Your guys are giving me hemorrhoids."

Tice went to the old standby again in the 2003 offseason. Tice admitted he was getting uptight when the team was slow in adding defensive backs. But he celebrated when the team signed top cornerback Denard Walker.

"I think my hemorrhoids have calmed down," Tice said in front of the cameras in Walker's introductory press conference.

"I know, I know, TMI," he later said.

Mike Tice: The Vikings' head coach is known for his legendary temper. A day of practice rarely goes by without Tice raising his deep voice. (Photo by Rick A. Kolodziej)

THE HORSEMAN

Before he was a football coach, Tice was a racehorse owner. He has studied championship thoroughbreds and learned their tendencies, and he has applied that information and knowledge to football players.

He believes in the confidence factor. Horses, as well as football players, lose confidence as their production declines.

"You could have a really nice horse, and in its first race it may finish in the middle of the pack and feel good about itself," Tice explains. "Then, in the horse's second race, it could finish fifth or sixth. And then, in its third race, the horse will finish dead last. Well, the horse will sense it is not improving and will lose its confidence. That horse will never, ever win a race. It's true. I've seen it happen. That's why I won't let it happen to my young players."

As a result, Tice is notoriously quick with the hook when it comes to young players. He wants his players to realize they're struggling before it's too late.

Seventeen players lost their starting jobs in Tice's first season.

"I see things we aren't doing right, and I study for solutions," Tice said. "This week, we're working on pass protection on the offensive line, doing drills we haven't done all season, because we need to . . . What is the key to coaching? I think it's adjustments. You have to make adjustments during the game and you have to make adjustments during the week as well."

THE DARKER SIDE

Tice was well known for his verbal explosions as offensive line coach. Rarely a week would go by without his players incurring the wrath of Tice. The preseason was just one game old in Tice's tenure as head coach when the rest of the squad realized what the linemen had gone through the past five years.

Two days after a sloppy performance in the preseason opener, Tice welcomed his players back from a day off with a long, loud and pointed team meeting.

During the meeting, Tice showed the team what center Matt Bark called a "lowlight film" of the team's 27-15 loss to Cleveland. Tice spliced together film of players making mental and physical errors, and he harped on the importance of making corrections.

"He showed his darker side," right tackle Chris Liwienski said. "It was nothing new to the O-linemen. We're used to it. Today, though, the entire team saw it."

Defensive back Corey Chavous, in his first season with the team, said it was good for young players to see their coach show his passion.

"Coach Tice had a point to make, and I believe he did an excellent job of bringing it home," Chavous said. "We got what he was telling us. We have to get better, and after that meeting, we all knew it."

TICE IS MR. SEATTLE

The Seahawks entered the NFL along with the Tampa Bay Buccaneers in 1976. Like most expansion teams, the Seahawks struggled on the field and were trying to find a personality and an identity in the Pacific Northwest.

As the team stumbled into the 1980s, it was still looking for a presence. Mike Tice, who was with the Seahawks from 1981-88 and '90-91, came along. He was big, hard-working and full of life. He opened his giant arms and embraced the city.

"The organization really grew along with Mike," said Seahawks vice president of communications Gary Wright, who has been with the franchise since its inception. "Mike really helped the Seahawks come into their own. He helped create the excitement that surrounded the team in the early 1980s."

Tice, who developed into a solid NFL tight end after coming to the team as a weak-throwing quarterback, was one of the most quotable players in the newspapers and was a constant presence on television. He loved to spread the word about the team and was available at any time.

"We could be at any event in the community, and Mike was willing to do anything," Wright said. "He was one of the most reliable players we ever had. You could always count on Mike Tice. If we had a player bail out on us or if there was an emergency, Mike was available. We'd be at the event itself and call Mike, and he'd show. He loved being a Seattle Seahawk."

SEATTLE TRIP

Mike Tice spent 10 years of his NFL career in Seattle. He said it's the place where he became a man. He and his wife, Diane, still have an off-season home in the Seattle area and plan to settle down there.

When the Vikings made a trip to Seattle in Tice's first year with the team, more than 75 friends and family attended the game. Diane Tice hosted a huge preseason tailgate party. In fact, more people were in the Tice party in Seattle than were at the team's game at the New York Jets, three weeks later. Surprising, considering Tice is from New York.

"Seattle is home," Tice said. "It's a special place."

FILL YOUR BELLY DELI

Two years after joining the team, Mike and Diane Tice brought a piece of their home to Seattle. They opened a New York-style restaurant in the suburb of Redmond. In step with Tice's quirky and humorous side, the establishment was called The Fill Your Belly Deli.

"Mike had the best pastrami sandwiches this side of the Mississippi River," said family friend Tom Everhart, who met the Tices because he was a transplant drawn to the food of his native New York.

Diane and her sister Joanne cooked much of the food (Diane was known for her homemade cookies) and worked at the counter. Mike Tice would often work at the deli, which was adorned with autographed pictures of Tice's friends from around the NFL.

"That place was a congregating spot for players and fans alike," former Seattle safety Eugene Robinson said. "I remember during the strike year [1987] all the players would hang out at The Fill Your Belly Deli ... Mike's food kept us all together."

LURCH

Mike Tice was a favorite of his teammates in Seattle, who called the six-foot-eight tight end "Lurch." But as former teammate Steve Raible said now that Tice made it to the ranks of head coach, he tended to be referred to as "Mr. Lurch."

"Mike was a leader," Eugene Robinson said. "He was friends with everyone. He kept the locker room together and loose. Old Ticer was a great one."

TICE THE QUARTERBACK

Jim Zorn and Steve Largent—the star quarterback and receiver of the upstart Seahawks—were standing on the sideline during a May minicamp in 1981. They saw a shadow emerge from the locker room. This massive form was wearing a Seahawks uniform. It was—"Lurch."

"Well, [that's] Mr. Lurch now that he's a head coach," former Seattle receiver Steve Raible said.

Zorn and Largent were stunned to see this young player pick up a football.

"That was the biggest quarterback I've ever seen," Zorn said. "He couldn't throw the ball very well, but he had great desire."

Zorn said Tice, who called himself a blocking quarterback at the University of Maryland, impressed the veteran players when he knew he wasn't going to make it as a quarterback but still wouldn't give up.

"I'll never forget seeing Tice for the first time," Seattle quarterback Jim Zorn related. "He came out and bounced balls all over the place. It was pretty clear we had a great blocking tight end on our hands.

"Mike asked to become a tight end even though he never played the position," Zorn said. "This was a man who knew he could contribute to the team. ... We knew this was a football player then."

SCHOOL SPIRIT

Mike Tice is a proud alumnus of the University of Maryland. He often boasts of being a Terrapin and tries to catch the school playing football and basketball as often as possible.

Tice cherishes his time in College Park. He also loves being around folks from the school.

In 2003, when the Vikings wanted a veteran, experienced backup to Daunte Culpepper, Tice targeted Neil O'Donnell. He fit every criteria Tice wanted in a mentor for Culpepper. The fact that O'Donnell went to Maryland was a bonus.

"You gotta to love his choice of colleges," Tice said. "We need as many former Maryland quarterbacks on the roster as possible."

To help lasso O'Donnell in, Tice called on the four coaches on his staff with Maryland ties to take O'Donnell out to dinner. They did allow one outsider—offensive coordinator and Idaho alum Scott Linehan—to join them.

"We still made him sing the Maryland fight song," Tice joked.

PLAYERS STAND BEHIND THEIR COACH

Tight end Hunter Goodwin returned to the Vikings after a four-year absence because he wanted to win with Mike Tice.

After the Vikings started the season 0-4, Goodwin believed the team had let down its first-year coach.

"It makes me sick," Goodwin said. "This has been the worst four weeks of my life, and it's so frustrating because you want to win for coach Tice. Guys are going crazy because they know he's doing all the right things.

"I've been in some pretty good programs under Dennis Green, Jimmy Johnson and Dave Wannstedt, and Mike Tice's program is just as strong as any of theirs. We just have to turn it around for him. And we will; he's got us behind him all the way."

"Coach Tice is the reason why we believe," Byron Chamberlain said. "He's got us feeling good about ourselves, and that's not easy when a team is 0-4. It shows what a true leader he is."

PEOPLE PERSON

Mike Tice is a man of the people. Perhaps Tice's greatest passion—besides coaching, of course—is meeting Vikings fans. During a day at training camp in 2002, Tice took advantage of an afternoon off by going to a Mankato shopping mall to sign autographs at a women's clothing store.

The line snaked past several stores and was about three hundred people deep. Tice catered to the fans. If the fan had ten items to be autographed, he signed them all. He greeted every fan with a smile and some type of comment. These weren't canned conversations. Every fan had a new greeting and was asked something different.

Posing with a small boy, the six-foot-eight Tice looked down on the intimidated child and said, "Boy, you're tall," instantly disarming the little man.

"These people are the reason why I'm the coach of the Vikings," Tice said. "Giving them a smile and some kind words is the least I can do."

A DAY IN THE LIFE

Training camp days are long, tiring, mundane. One day runs into the next. For Tice, this exercise in repetition begins at 6 a.m. and ends at 2 a.m.

Tice gets up, eats a banana, exercises, works on his computer, meets with staff, talks to the strength coaches, meets with the team's medical staff—and then the day starts.

After these chores, Tice gets ready to coach the team. After a two and half-hour practice, Tice eats lunch, meets with his coaches, watches film and then heads out to the afternoon practice.

Then, it's dinner, meetings, coaching film sessions, and another team meeting followed by a film session in his dorm suite with the coaches.

"It's a 20-hour day that flies by in five minutes," Tice said. "Before I know it, it's the next day again. So let's do it again."

THE MENTOR

One of the treats of training camp for Tice was when his coach in Seattle, Chuck Knox Sr., came to camp for a week. His son, Chuck Knox Jr., is the Vikings' defensive backs coach.

Knox—known for his quick wit—brought levity to camp. He spent long evenings laughing and reminiscing with the coaches. Tice also had Knox address the team, becoming sheepish when Knox told the players a tale of when he was the Seahawks' coach and Tice was a wild tight end.

Knox told his Seattle players that he knew three players had broke curfew one night in training camp. He said all three of the players had to fess up or every player would be fined. Six players, however, admitted to staying out too late, surprising Knox.

"I missed three guys," Knox said.

Guess who one of those extra three players was? The Vikings head coach.

"I could have gotten away with one," Tice said, laughing. "I hope Coach Knox didn't give my players any ideas."

BASEBALL DAD

How did Mike Tice celebrate the arrival of his first training camp as a head coach?

By coaching his son's youth baseball team, of course. By pure coincidence, the Edina, Minn., All-Star team of 13-year-olds, which included cousins Nate Tice and Michael Tice, the son of John Tice, Mike's brother and the Vikings tight ends coach, had a game in Mankato, Minn., the night the Vikings reported for camp in 2002.

So Tice had a short team meeting and then headed out to coach the game. John Tice, as with the Vikings, was his older brother's assistant coach on the diamond.

Could you imagine hard-boiled coaches Bill Parcells or Jon Gruden coaching kids the day before camp started?

Tice's commitment to children continued during the season when he helped coach his son's football team. "We won the championship," Tice said during the 2002 season.

"So at least I know I can win at some level," he said jokingly.

A LITTLE BIT OF EVERYONE

When he was hired at the tender age of 42, Tice said he wouldn't pattern his coaching style after one man, but several. Tice has taken something from all of the pivotal men in his career.

Tice took knowledge from Knox, Joe Gibbs, for whom he played in Washington, and Dennis Green, for whom he played and coached with the Vikings.

"They all taught me something, so I'm using things from all of them," Tice said. "I've been extremely lucky to work for and with great football men. I might as well take advantage of it and meld all of their knowledge and greatness together and try to make it mine."

RULES ARE RULES

While Tice likes to joke and have a good time, he's all business when it comes to the workday. When he took over for Green, Tice made several rules.

Among them were no cell phones allowed in the locker room or meeting rooms, and he made all the players eat their meals in the lunchroom to build camaraderie.

In the past, players were able to eat at their lockers or in the player lounge.

"This is a job and they will treat it that way," Tice said. "Rules are rules, and it will make us a better, more close-knit team."

A SERENE PLACE

Mike Tice's office at Winter Park is more New Age than old-school NFL.

In fact, a look at the office and one would think they were in a spa, not the office of a head coach in the NFL.

Sure, there are the requisite trophies displayed and football photos on the wall, but Tice's office also has a splash of modern comfort. Tice has a soothing waterfall that hangs over his desk and slowly drips water. His CD player often plays classical music.

Tice is an admittedly high-strung person. He gets uptight. But as a renowned yeller, Tice still finds his quiet time.

His office serves as his escape.

"I need my space to chill out," Tice said. "This place does it. It calms me and sometimes I need to clam down. You look at the little waterfall and that does it. I'm at peace when I'm in here."

FAMILY FIRST

While Tice spends most of his time during the season at Winter Park, he tries to work in as much family quality time as possible. But he often has to be creative.

He had to squeeze in time for his daughter Adrian's 15th birthday at a Mankato pizza parlor in between camp practices. His son Nate was a ball boy during training camp and stayed with his father in his dorm suite.

Diane Tice also brought their kids to several road games.

"The biggest thing to Coach Tice is his family," assistant Todd Downing said.

"No matter how busy he is during the season, he tries to sneak in as much family time as possible."

THE NEW YORKER

Mike Tice isn't afraid of making bold statements.

The brash New Yorker loves to talk and isn't afraid to step out on a limb. When the season-ending press conference cameras were rolling on December 30, 2002, Tice didn't bat an eye.

"We're going to go to the playoffs, I'll tell you that right now," Tice deadpanned.

Tice dropped that bombshell less than 24 hours after he departed the victorious visitor's locker room in Detroit by saying the team would reverse their record and finish at least 10-6 next season.

Later that day, Tice didn't back off his promise that the team would end its two-season playoff drought.

"We're going to get there," said Tice, whose team won its final three games to finish 6-10. "We're not far off at all, just some tweaking."

Chapter 8

Korey Stringer

BIG K

Korey Stringer was one of the most well-liked and well-respected players ever to play for the Vikings.

He grew from a fun-loving boy into a responsible successful man right in front of the organization's eyes. Stringer was an overweight 21-year-old who didn't know his own potential when the Vikings took a chance on him by taking him in the first round of the 1995 draft.

So many teams passed on Stringer. It was agreed amongst scouts that he had uncanny size, strength and ability, but almost no one thought the right tackler was worth it.

The Vikings did, though, and Stringer became well worth their while.

Stringer flourished with the Vikings. He got his weight under control and realized that with his abilities he could become one of the most dominant players at his position.

He reached his potential in 2000 when he was named to the NFC Pro Bowl team, which had long been his dream.

When he found out he was named to play the game in Hawaii, he first called his mother, Kathy. It was her birthday, and playing in the game was his gift to her.

It was the final game of his life.

Stringer died August 1, 2001, of heatstroke after collapsing during practice. He received medical attention for 14 straight hours before passing away at 1:50 A.M. at a Mankato hospital. Stringer was 27 years old.

HAD TO STAY STRONG

Kelci Stringer amazed the nation with her unwavering strength in the months after she became a widow. Stringer, who has retained a publicist, has been on several national news shows and has spoken eloquently about her husband's life and death. She admits she isn't always that strong.

"Sometimes when I'm talking publicly I don't think I'm being fair to Korey because I'm talking about an aspect of his life that really didn't matter to us," she said. "I talk about him the football player and the public figure. But we didn't talk about personal stuff. I mean this was a guy who painted my toenails for me. It was a very personal relationship. And to keep talking about the Korey people really didn't know, I feel like I'm cheating Korey."

Stringer said she surprised herself over how composed she was in the immediate days and months after her husband's death. She said it was about December that she began to succumb to her grief.

"I wish I still had that peace I originally had," she said. "I knew it wouldn't last, but it sure helped me at the beginning. I still feel like I'm strong, but I have my moments."

TOUGH DAY

One of the most poignant moments after Korey Stringer's death was a press conference conducted by then coach Dennis Green and star receivers Cris Carter and Randy Moss. It was held nine hours after Stringer's death, and all three men were sleep deprived and under great distress.

All three men broke down on the stage. Several media members—there were more than a hundred reporters in the Mankato State gymnasium—were clearly moved. Members of owner Red McCombs's family, sitting in the front row, were crying.

"This is a very tough time," Carter said. "It's hard to put into words."

SAYING GOODBYE

One goodbye wasn't enough to say goodbye to a man as loved as Korey Stinger. Two days after his death, the Vikings held a private memorial service in Edina, Minn. The funeral was attended by every player and their companions, the coaching staff, and most of the organization.

Tice spoke, as well as several other players, including close friends Randy Moss, Mitch Berger and David Dixon. Moss passed around a Stringer No. 77 jersey for everyone in the service to touch.

"We miss you, Big K," said a choked-up Moss.

Three days later, Moss and several teammates attended Stringer's service in his hometown of Warren, Ohio. Dennis Green and Tice represented the coaching staff at the funeral, which more than 500 people attended, including several NFL players who knew and played against Stringer.

*Korey Stringer: Big K was beloved by his teammates
and coaches. Mike Tice called Stringer his "baby."
(Photo by Rick A. Kolodziej)*

THEY CAME OUT FOR KOREY

More than a hundred former teammates of Stringer's came to the Twin Cities to see him inducted into the ring of honor and to see his massive No. 77 forever be retired.

The event was enough to bring the reclusive Robert Smith back to Minnesota for the first time since his surprise retirement nine months earlier.

"We all had to come back for this," said former linebacker Pete Bercich, a teammate of Stringer's for six years. "Korey was a favorite. His death hurt us all. We all needed to be here for this, to honor him one last time."

THE TREE OF MEMORY

Two weeks after Korey Stringer died, the Vikings and Minnesota State-Mankato came together to plant a tree in front of the team's dormitory, Gage Hall, in Stringer's memory. At the base of the tree is a plaque memorializing Stringer.

Several players joined coach Dennis Green to dig a hole for the tree.

The tree has become a wonderful reminder of Stringer. Players pass by it every day during training camp. As the tree grows, players get strength from it and enjoy good thoughts about their lost friend.

"I look at the tree a lot," said David Dixon, Stringer's training camp roommate. "That tree is memories."

REPLACING KOREY

When it was time to think about football again, no name was more connected to Korey Stringer than Chris Liwienski's.

Liwienski had to replace Stringer on the field as the Vikings' right tackle. He had to replace a mentor and a friend.

"Looking back on that challenge, it was extremely difficult," Liwienski said. "Not the football part, but just the idea of taking over for Korey. Nobody could take over for Korey. He was in a league of his own. But the game had to go on. The league wasn't going to end the season for us.

"I remember the night after he died, it was such a bad day, and coach Tice came in and told me I was at right tackle now. It was like, OK, I have to go do this for Korey."

A FRIEND AND A FOE

Packers defensive tackle Santana Dotson knew something was different when he hit the Metrodome turf in the fall of 2001. Korey Stringer wasn't there. Sadness overwhelmed Dotson.

"Yeah, the big fella will be missed," Dotson said. "He was a big part of what the Vikings did. It's tough to know he won't be there."

"I just knew him from the field and had some really spirited battles with him," Dotson said of the Pro Bowl right tackle. "The only real words I had with him were four-letter words on the field, but I really respected him."

THE BABY

Mike Tice called all of his offensive linemen his "babies." He called Korey Stringer his son.

"Everyone thought Matt Birk was my number one son," said the Vikings' head coach and former offensive lineman. "But Korey was my number one son."

When Korey Stringer died, Mike Tice cried.

"Losing Korey was the toughest thing in my life," Tice said. "I lost my favorite baby and my son."

FUNNY MAN

Korey Stringer made everyone laugh. He usually did it by making fun of you. No one was immune. Teammates, coaches, media. Anyone that came in this massive man's path would pay for it.

Gently, of course.

Stringer was a wicked impersonator. Rich Little would be proud.

"It just takes a little while," he once said. "All I have to do is listen to someone talk for a few minutes. And I can nail it."

"Korey could do anybody's voice," added defensive back Robert Griffith, a close friend. "He was a comedian. He should have been in Hollywood."

Stringer's favorite target of impersonation was Mike Tice, one of the closest people to him in his life. Stringer found Tice's deep baritone voice sprinkled with a New York accent irresistible.

"He could do Coach Tice like he was Coach Tice," Griffith said. "He was perfect."

GREAT DOGS

In the offensive line meeting rooms, when he wasn't singing or perfectly reciting lines from his favorite movie, Korey Stringer would tell his teammates and coaches about his hometown of Warren, Ohio. He told them about his high school, his neighborhood, the people he knew and his favorite restaurant. It was a hot dog joint that he absolutely loved.

Tice and Dean Dalton, then his assistant offensive line coach, found themselves staying up late into the night, reminiscing about Stringer.

The chats would come back to Warren and those hot dogs.

One day after visiting the Stringer family, Vikings support staff member Sid Pillai brought Tice and Dalton a gift back from Warren.

"Korey was right," Dalton said. "Those hot dogs were great."

THE HANDS

What made Korey Stringer so effective on the field was those gigantic hands. His hands were enormous. They were the size of a Little Leaguer's catcher's mitt. When you shook the hand of Korey Stringer, you instantly felt your hand engulfed by a greater being. It was as if you suddenly had an infant's hand.

Stringer put those big, long, porterhouse steak-thick hands to great use on the football field. He manhandled defensive linemen who tried to get past him. Stringer would simply hook his hands onto the defender and stop him in his tracks.

"I played against him and practiced against him and I never experienced anything like it," former teammate John Burrough said. "Those hands were so strong. Korey's hands made him so hard and so unfun to play against."

Added Tice: "It was the hands that made him special. He had great strength in those hands. It made him a cut above."

A HUGE HEART

One of the stories that best defined Korey Stringer emerged in the days following his death.

The week before he died, Stringer visited his hometown and met with several friends. One of the friends he visited with ran the city's Pop Warner football program.

The friend mentioned in passing to Stringer, a product of the program himself, that the organization had some budget problems and was going to have a difficult time getting new uniforms and equipment for the upcoming season.

Stringer listened and then walked out to his truck. Moments later, he appeared with a $10,000 check. It was his paycheck from the NFC Pro Bowl team the winter before. Without saying anything, he signed it over to the league for the equipment and left.

His friend never saw him again. But the Pop Warner league played with new equipment that fall.

Chapter 9

Red McCombs and the Fans

AMONG THE BEST

The Vikings fans are known for being wild and loyal. Along with fans in Denver, Green Bay and Oakland, the Vikings fans are considered among the very best in the NFL.

There's plenty of proof to back it up. There is a waiting list with thousands of names on it. Plus, the Vikings are traditionally around the league's leader in merchandise sold. The Vikings are one of the few teams whose fan base goes beyond their region. It is not unusual to see Vikings fans at every road game. At training camp, fans converged on Mankato from all over the country. Several fans from the California Vikings Fan Club spend their summer vacations in Southern Minnesota watching their favorite team train.

"It's great to see these fans out in the heat with us at camp," running back Michael Bennett said. "They are there early in the morning and it gives us strength."

*Red McCombs: The flamboyant Texan was a big presence at games
after he bought the Vikings. If you say "hello" to the car dealer,
you'll always get a hearty "Purple Pride" in return.
(Photo courtesy of Jonathan Daniel/Getty Images)*

GREAT SUPPORT

The Vikings realized the strength of their passionate fan base at the end of their disappointing 2002 season. The Vikings were mired in a poor season, which ended with a game at Detroit. The game pitted the 5-10 Vikings and the 3-12 Lions. Of the 16 NFL games that weekend, the Vikings-Lions game was just one of four that didn't have playoff implications. It was one of the wildest final NFL weekends in memory. Playoff fever was abounding. But for the Vikings and Lions, they were simply finishing out the slate at the new Ford Field in downtown Detroit.

Still, stunningly, the television rating in Minnesota for the game was through the roof.

"Vikings fans are the best," owner Red McCombs said. "They watched us at home and on television. They can't get enough of the Vikings even when things aren't going great. These are the best fans in the league."

SAYING THANKS

Inspired by a letter to the editor of a Minnesota newspaper, Red McCombs purchased full-page advertisements in both Twin Cities newspapers. The ads thanked a Bloomington, Minn., fan for her kind words. In her letter, the fan thanked the Vikings for their hard work and their unwillingness to lie down in a season in which the team started 3-10 but rallied to win their three final games. In the ad, McCombs thanked the fan and said all the Vikings have great attitudes.

"I'm inspired by fans," McCombs said. "They keep us going."

SIGN TIME

Mike Tice decided to have a little fun with the team and Vikings fans one day during the dog days of training camp. It was early August, and the team was caught up in a string of several days of back-to-back double day practices.

So to break up the monotony of camp, Tice decided to give both his players and the loyal fans who came out in 90-degree weather a treat. At the beginning of the afternoon practice, it seemed like business as usual. Tice had the players get in their full uniform and the team started its mundane but necessary stretching session. However, five minutes into the stretching, Tice had the grounds crew turn on the sprinklers, dousing the players, who all got up and ran for dry land.

The several hundred fans in the stands erupted in laughter. Tice then rounded up his wet players into a circle and told them they would have the rest of the day off. But because the fans came out to practice, Tice had every player sign autographs for a hour before departing.

"This gives everyone a nice break," Tice said. "The players have worked hard and they deserve time off and the fans come out here for autographs and they deserve those. So everyone is happy even though they're a little wet."

PURPLE PRIDE

Mike Tice will answer his office phone a few times a week and hear a loud, bellowing Texas-sized voice on the other end.

"Purple Pride," yells owner Red McCombs.

Tice laughs each time.

"Red doesn't have to identify himself," Tice said. "I know exactly who it is with that twangy 'Purple Pride.' Red loves his Purple Pride."

The two-word phase became the Vikings' battle cry when McCombs bought the team in 1998. McCombs wears a purple shirt and matching blazer to nearly every team function. He made the "Purple Pride" his own greeting immediately after buying the team. Now the mantra is on team stationery and is ever-present at the Metrodome.

"It's my way of showing team unity," McCombs said. "Every Vikings coach, player, employee and fan has to have Purple Pride. That's how we're going to get it done."

Chapter 10

Fun and Games

GOT MILK?

Football players are, obviously, competitive. Give a football player a challenge and he'll do his best to meet it—even if it's off the field, extremely difficult, or sometimes really silly.

Such was the case during the late 1990s on a lazy Friday afternoon. The practice day breaks early on Fridays, so players are usually rambunctious as the work week comes to a close and game day approaches.

On this particular Friday, several veteran players made a friendly bet with young running back Obafemi Ayanbadejo that he couldn't drink a large jug of milk—and keep it down. The fun-loving kid they called—"Femi" was confident, though.

He was sure he could chug the milk and keep it down. He was right about one part. Ayanbadejo easily downed the cold jug of milk. That was the easy part.

But the milk didn't exactly stay down.

The veterans howled in laughter. Ayanbadejo, though, like a true football player was stunned that he lost the competition.

YOU SHOULDN'T HAVE SAID THAT

The unwritten rule amongst NFL players is that kickers and punters must know their place. Basically, it means they must keep their mouths shut.

In 1989, Rich Karlis broke the golden rule of a kicker. He opened his mouth. Making the mistake even worse was that he was opening his mouth in protest of an offensive lineman. That's a big no-no in an NFL locker room.

Karlis thought he was clever when he called the Vikings' offensive linemen slobs and said they didn't know how to dress. He was joking, but still, the damage was done, especially since one of Karlis's targets was center Kirk Lowdermilk, his own brother-in-law. The family ties didn't aid Karlis in obtaining a free pass.

The offensive linemen vowed revenge. It didn't take long for them to strike against the mouthy kicker.

One Saturday, after the team wrapped up a walkthrough practice, the offensive linemen converged on Karlis. They savagely took him to a goal post and taped him to it. Upside down.

The non-clotheshorses left Karlis to fend for himself. Lowdermilk was a ringleader in the upheaval.

REINDEER GAMES

In the early and mid-1990s the Vikings' locker room could be a rowdy, raucous place. Some said it resembled a fraternity house.

It was a good bet that most of the nonsense being created was from the offensive linemen. The group—led by Randall McDaniel, Jeff Christy, Mike Morris and Todd Steussie—was known for having a little fun, or as some observers said—"they were always around playing their reindeer games."

If there was any mischief going on, it was usually coming from one of the Vikings' hogs. One of the ringleaders of the offensive line pranksters was McDaniel. A quiet man, his favorite goof was placing a stink bomb in the players' restrooms. An unsuspecting player would use the facilities and then come running out, gasping for air and overwhelmed by the horrible fumes.

And in their corner, McDaniel and the other "reindeer" would be doubled over in laughter.

HAPPY HOLIDAYS

One of the more free-spirited Vikings of all time was offensive lineman David Huffman, who played for the team from 1979-83 and then '85-90. The late Huffman is still fondly remembered at Winter Park for his fun-loving antics. He was always the life of the party.

Huffman couldn't be accused of not trying to spread his own brand of Christmas cheer. After all, it's the thought that counts.

One early December, Huffman shocked his teammates

Randall McDaniel: The offensive lineman was known for making his mark on the field with his tough play and in the players' restrooms with his well-placed stink bombs. (Photo courtesy of Stephen Dunn/Getty Images)

when he emerged wearing only a jock strap and a muffler. He then proceeded outside to the snow-covered practice field for an impromptu photo shoot. The huge Huffman lay horizontally on the ground with his head resting on his shoulder. He had his Vikings helmet strategically placed in front of him for his modeling shoot.

Teammates and Vikings employees alike had no idea what Huffman was doing. That is, until they opened up their mailbox a few days later.

His photo was transformed into his Christmas card. The only inscription on the unique Christmas cheer was "And you thought I wouldn't write."

COLD PANTS

Rookie Kelly Campbell was often the life of the Vikings' party during his rookie year.

After the season finale of the 2002 season, several teammates good-naturedly tired of the little man's big mouth. So, in the midst of the victorious locker room at Detroit's Ford Field, someone took Campbell's underwear out of his locker and threw it into the shower.

Campbell's squeals bounced off all the corners of the locker room walls when he realized he'd have to go home with wet underwear.

"That's what you get, rookie," yelled Moss, with a hearty laugh.

Campbell kept everyone in the organization on edge with his boisterous behavior.

"Kelly is a great kid, but he'll do anything for a laugh," said a front-office member. "If we win the Super Bowl and go visit the White House, Kelly is liable to moon the president for kicks."

ROCKET MAN

Perhaps Elton John was singing about Jim Marshall in "Rocket Man?"

In addition to being one of the fiercest, most reliable players in the NFL, the Vikings' star defensive end was also the Rocket Man.

During the dog days of training camp, the Vikings players got rather creative in how they would spend their free time. During a couple of training camps, the players were on an outer space kick. So a bunch of players would go to a local hobby shop and buy toy rockets that actually shot upward into the air.

Of course, the competitive players would bet on whose rocket would go higher.

One day, Marshall—the leader of this competition— brought a three-foot-tall rocket that towered over all the other smaller, sleeker, and more aerodynamic rockets.

Marshall had a secret weapon. So he took all kinds of bets form skeptical amateur rocket scientists who didn't think the big clunker could get airborne.

No one knew that Marshal, who'd always wore a Red Baron hat to the festivities, put a frog in the rocket to give it extra jumping power. True story.

"But the word got out that Marshal was using a frog," Bob Lurtsema said. "He called it Freddie the Frog. Pretty ingenious, huh? And it worked.

"That rocket made it up in the air, all right," Lurtsema said. "Jim won all the bets … But no one ever saw the frog again. I guess Freddie the Frog was sacrificed for the greater good."

SHOWING YOUR CARDS

One of the favorites of the many non-football pastimes during training camp for the Vikings of the 1970s was poker games during lunch hour.

The stakes weren't high, but they were enough to get the players' competitive spirits going and to make eating a secondary priority of the hour.

"We choked down our food as soon as possible," defensive end Bob Lurtsema said. "Eating wasn't the goal. Winning at cards was the goal."

Players would huddle in a dorm room and play as many hands as possible. Lurtsema said about 10 players would play and guys would leave as soon as they won a pot.

Trainer Fred Zamberletti always knew which players won and lost. The players who won were in the training room getting taped for the afternoon practice on time. The losers were staying behind as long as possible trying to win.

"It would always come down to the two losers trying to win at least one jackpot," Lurtsema said. "Freddie always laughed at the losers. Sometimes, guys would run right from the card room to the practice field and not get taped because it took them too long to win."

BOCCI, ANYONE?

Was this a cruise ship or an NFL training camp?

Cards, social hour and bocci ball? Yes, the Vikings played some wicked games of bocci ball in their free time during training camp.

Longtime trainer Freddie Zamberletti introduced the game to the players and they would engage in the sport near the practice field in the free time during the evening. Many players participated in the Italian game with Zamberletti. Players such as Paul Krause, Jim Marshall and Doug Sutherland excelled at the game.

"It got to the point where football was the furthest thing from our mind," joked Bob Lurtsema. "It was all about bocci ball … We'd be at practice, tired as a dog and panting. But we'd muster up the strength to look at each other and say, 'I'm going to kick your butt in bocci ball tonight.' We were just little kids playing games."

SHOTGUN START

Jim Marshall was the starter.

Players couldn't do much without their leader's approval, and that included leaving Mankato for preseason games. Coach Bud Grant allowed players to drive themselves from Mankato to The Met for preseason games. The players got the evening off as well as the day after the game, so Grant allowed the players to provide their own transportation to the game.

But Grant, still trying to keep some of his trademark structure, wouldn't allow the players to depart training camp until 1:30 p.m. and they had to go straight to the stadium. Still, no one could leave until Marshall said so. He had a unique way of letting everyone know it was go time.

"Guys would be mulling around for hours just waiting for Jim to shoot the gun," Lurtsema said.

"Jim would come out to the parking lot of our dorm and all the guys would be in their cars, just waiting," Lurtsema said. "Then he'd pull out this big pistol and shoot it in the air. Guys would go wild and then hit the road.

"Jim was our starter. We didn't do anything until the gun came out."

PARADE DAY

The team's trip up Highway 169 to the Met would be escorted by police, and fans would line the highway to get a glimpse of their favorite players driving by. Fans on their way to the game knew when the team was leaving and arrange their plans to be part of the caravan.

"It was special," Lurtsema said. "It was just a preseason game but they all made it seem like the Super Bowl. It got us pumped up. Kids would be hanging out the back of the cars and waving Vikings flags. It was a huge parade to The Met."

GAME TIME

As if playing a child's game for a living isn't enough, several Vikings played board games in their down time during the day. The two most popular games are dominoes and cribbage.

In a small player's lounge off the locker room, several players play loud, competitive games of dominoes. Over the years, the most ardent dominoes players have included Randy Moss, Orlando Thomas, Ed McDaniel and David Dixon. The primary cribbage players are Matt Birk, Chris Walsh, Everett Lindsay and Chris Liwienski.

"You gotta pass time somehow," Birk said. "We get some pretty hardcore games going."

ON THE HUNT

Winter Park, the Vikings' practice facility that sits right off Interstate 494 in Eden Prairie, is an attraction for fans. Perhaps drawn by the large Viking ship that's displayed in front of the facility, fans often drop by to take pictures and perhaps to try to sneak a peek of a player or two.

However, sometimes folks come on a mission.

One winter's night, several University of Minnesota co-eds emerged from the parking lot. They were obviously on a sorority scavenger hunt.

The mission: Get your picture taken with a real-life Minnesota Viking. It didn't take the students long to accomplish their goal.

As soon as they sprinted near the locker room, affable defensive tackle Fred Robbins approached them as he was going to his car after a long day of work. The students quickly asked Robbins to pose for a picture. He did and then they were off as quickly as they arrived, to meet another hunt requirement.

Chapter 11

The Elements

THE MET

For the first half of the Vikings' existence, when you thought of the Vikings you formed an instant mental image of Metropolitan Stadium in Bloomington.

Wrigley Field has the ivy; the Boston Garden had the parquet floors. The Met had freezing players in purple uniforms breathing cold air out of their helmets.

The Met was well known for hosting some of the coldest games in league history. You want a home-field advantage? Just go to the Met in December. No one had a chance.

"You get a team from the South and they wouldn't know what to do in that cold," said former coach Jerry Burns, who was a Vikings assistant from 1968-85. "Teams weren't used to that cold. It was our thing. We played and strived in the cold."

Even though it was a great advantage, the Vikings decided to get a little modern and move inside for the 1982 season, ending a 20-year run at The Met.

The Metrodome: In 1982 the Vikings moved indoors. Thanks to the Metrodome's acoustics, it's one of the noisiest NFL stadiums. (Photo courtesy AP/WWP)

"The Metrodome has been great," Bob Lurtsema said. "But the Met was a nasty place to play for opponents. They weren't used to it. We were and really liked playing even in the cold. We were the Vikings and the Vikings loved playing outside in the Old Met. I still miss that place even though I get cold thinking of it."

COLD WEATHER

The equipment managers are usually known for several things: hard work, always being on the go, and being a little to the left of center.

In Minnesota, equipment manager Dennis Ryan and his trusty sidekick Aaron Neumann are known for their hard, diligent work. However, they are also known for not minding the cold weather. In fact, the two native Minnesotans crave it.

Traditionally, they start aching for snow in September and are quick to chide folks who are bundled up—even in the dead of winter. They, of course, do their chiding in nothing but shorts and T-shirts. Always. They would wear shorts in outside winter games if it was allowed, but it's against team policy to wear shorts on game day.

On a 20-degree day in December, the team conducted a rare outside practice to prepare for a December night game in Green Bay. Everyone was bundled up, except Ryan and Neumann. The two scurried around the practice field in their customary white T-shirts and purple shorts. As Ryan came running onto the field, Randy Moss stopped in his tracks and shook his head.

"What's the problem?" Ryan asked. "It's not cold out here."

STILL NOT READY FOR THE COLD

Even though the Vikings play and live in Minnesota—perhaps the coldest NFL territory—they are not used to playing in cold weather. In fact, the Vikings are about as unprepared as the Miami Dolphins or Dallas Cowboys to play in cold-weather games.

Think about it. They practice inside; they play inside. The only time the Vikings are in the winter elements is when they walk to their cars to and from practice.

"I don't like the cold like anyone else," defensive tackle Chris Hovan said. "We're in it as little as possible."

NO BENCH WARMERS

One of the favorite pastimes of former players is saying how much the game has changed and how tough they had it back in their days of the gridiron.

Well, when you hear the Vikings who called the Met their home, you may want to listen. It's not just rhetoric when they talked about their hard times. Well, make that their cold times.

The contemporary Vikings, who enjoy the comfort of the Metrodome, never had to deal with the harsh cold of playing at the Met.

"The funniest part of the game today is these bench warmers they have," said Bob Lurtsema, who, ironically, had the nickname of "Benchwarmer Bob" when he played.

"I was at a game [in 2002] in Green Bay and it was a freezing cold night game in December and you should have seen the bench warmers they had," Lurtsema said. "It was very high tech. I couldn't believe it. We had nothing and liked it. All these guys are running about with warm buns. We had cold buns and we didn't know any better."

CHILLY NIGHT

To prepare his team for the first December night game in the history of Lambeau Field, coach Mike Tice had his team practice outside for the first time in almost a month despite the 25-degree weather. However, since they were two days away from playing in nine-degree weather, Tice had to get his troops ready for the elements.

In an attempt to simulate game-day conditions, Tice didn't allow his players to bring out sweatshirts or sweatpants. "Not even gloves, mittens or scarves were allowed," Tice said. "They had to get ready. It was all mental."

While the simulation helped, nothing prepared the team for the chilly evening elements.

"I don't think I sweated out there," left guard Corbin Lacina said. "It was the first game I've ever remembered that I didn't need a drink of water."

THE MET NO MORE?

The most famous shopping mall in the country now sits on a landfill of memories for Vikings and Twins fans.

When the Met was demolished in the early 1980s in favor of the Metrodome, there was a huge void in Bloomington just off Highway 494. It didn't sit empty for long, though. Soon, there was a development for the Mall of America, the biggest mall in the country.

So at the place where Fran Tarkenton scrambled, Jim Marshall sacked and Bud Grant schemed, now sits Camp Snoopy and a million different shoe stores.

"Sometimes I'm in the mall and try to figure where the playing field was," Bob Lurtsema said. "Being near a merry-go-round just doesn't seem like the same old Met to me."

FAMILY AFFAIR

The Met was basically one big family reunion. Ten times a year the Vikings and 60,000 of their closest friends would gather for a day at the ballpark.

Because the Twin Cities were so close-knit and because the Vikings were so beloved and became a fabric of the community, the players and fans became close. It was basically a big ol' high school game. After the game, players would join fans in the parking lot for tailgate parties and sign autographs.

"We'd play ball with the kids, tossing the ball around the parking lot," Bob Lurtsema said. "It was such a unique atmosphere. It would take me two hours to make my way out of that parking lot. What a great time."

THE NOISE

The Vikings have one of the best built-in home-field advantages. The combination of the acoustics inside the Metrodome and rabid fans makes for one of the noisiest stadiums in the NFL. In fact, the Vikings' public address announcer proudly proclaims that fact before every game.

There are several elements that make the Metrodome an ear-bleeding experience for visiting teams. There's the loud music that plays up to the snap of the ball, there's the rowdy team mascot revving up his motorcycle, and, of course, there's the constant roar of the fans.

*Mitch Berger: The strong-legged punter and kickoff specialist
was a fan favorite. When "Welcome to the Jungle" roared
throughout the stadium, you knew Berger was on the field.
(Photo courtesy of Jonathan Daniel/Getty Images)*

"That is not a great place to play," Green Bay defensive tackle Santana Dotson said. "It's just noise all the time. Whether it's the sound of the motorcycle or the fans, you leave that place with a big headache."

WELCOME TO THE JUNGLE

It got to the point where punter Mitch Berger almost became an honorary member of the rock group Guns 'N' Roses. Every time the strong-legged Berger prepared to kick off, the heavy metals band's signature song, "Welcome to the Jungle," would blare over the public address system. Thus, in 1998, when the Vikings set NFL scoring records, Guns 'N' Roses received more airplay than during their heyday.

Berger, who played for the Vikings from 1996-00, learned to love the song and the persona it helped to build for him. He became a favorite of young fans and did some correspondence work for rock stations in the Twin Cities. Even though the Vikings continued to use "Welcome to the Jungle" on kickoffs after Berger moved on, it was always associated with him.

"It's a cool thing," Berger said. "It sort of sets the tone for the noise and the aggression we want to establish. We think the Metrodome is the jungle."

Chapter 12

The End Zone

TWO-POINTER IN THE BAYOU

It was the call heard around the NFL. On Dec. 15, 2002, Vikings rookie coach Mike Tice went against conventional wisdom and common sense by calling for a two-point conversion instead of settling for overtime at New Orleans.

When the Vikings scored with five seconds remaining, making the score 31-30, they stunned the Superdome by keeping the offense on the field. Reserve receiver Chris Walsh jumped off the sideline, putting two fingers high into the air. The entire stadium buzzed with disbelief. Even the Vikings' front office members seated in the press box were stunned. They all stood up and erupted in nervous laughter.

"Sometimes you just go for it," said center Matt Birk, backing up his coach's gamble.

Tice later said he never thought twice. It was the right call. The Vikings were 3-10 and mired in a 17-game road losing streak that lasted 25 months. Tice said he had nothing to lose.

He felt even better when quarterback Daunte Culpepper fumbled a shotgun snap from Birk twice and still squirted into the end zone, converting the two-pointer and winning the game.

Coaches around the NFL lauded Tice for his incredible guts.

"Great call," San Francisco's Steve Mariucci said. "I don't know if I'd be able to call it, though."

THE UNSUNG HEROES

The equipment managers are well known as the hardest-working people in the organization. These dedicated workers are always the first people at Winter Park and the last to leave. It is not uncommon for them to bunk up at the facility because their workday went too late and the next workday was just a few hours away.

These workers are in charge of equipment, uniforms, setting up the practice field and transporting equipment to road games. Without them, the players and coaches would be lost. But they don't go without notice. They have been rewarded with game balls, and it's not uncommon for them to get the occasional tip from an appreciative player.

In his playing days, Scott Studwell would bring the equipment men biscuits every Saturday morning. As a player, Mike Tice would slip some cash into the coffee fund and Jack Del Rio bought one of the equipment managers a $100 bottle of champagne for his wedding.

"You have to take care of those guys," Tice said. "Without them there is no us. We'd be a mess."

*Scott Studwell: The intense Studwell has had a long
career with the Vikings, from his playing days as a standout
linebacker to his current job of heading up their college draft.
(Photo by Rick A. Kolodziej)*

SEND OUT THE DOGS

Bud Grant had a hard and fast rule for road games. He never wanted to arrive for a game early. He had it precisely planned that the Vikings' buses arrived at stadiums on the road an hour before games.

It would be just enough time for his players to dress and then hit the field for pregame warmups. Most teams did, and still do, arrive two hours before the game. But Grant didn't want his players to sit in the enemy's home with too much time on their hands. He wanted to cut it close so they'd be ready to go at kickoff.

But in Detroit in 1976 things didn't work out.

The Vikings were staying about 15 minutes away from the Silverdome in suburban Pontiac. They didn't realize just how bad traffic was on the way to the stadium. They soon found out. The Vikings buses—this was before the days of police escorts—got stuck in bumper-to-bumper traffic. Just like every other car on the highway, the Vikings were going to the game. Or, at least, trying to go to the game.

The buses didn't move for a half hour.

"It got pretty tense," then traveling secretary Jeff Diamond said, who went on to be the team's president. "I was on bus two and it was tense. I heard it was really tense on bus one where Coach Grant was."

Quarterback Fran Tarkenton tried to break the tension by running up and down the bus aisle. "He said it was his pregame warmups," Diamond said.

Finally, at about 12:55, the Vikings arrived at the Silverdome. Kickoff was in five minutes. Inside, the Silverdome was abuzz. Where were the Vikings?

"The league was upset, and you know the network was really upset," Diamond said.

The game was delayed by a half-hour. The league fined the Vikings $10,000 for causing the delay of game.

"Coach Grant didn't like being early," Diamond said. "But that was ridiculous. We were really rushed."

Still, the team wasn't rattled by their late arrival. They won the game 10-9.

STILL NOT RIGHT

With the memory of the year before still etched in everyone's minds, Jeff Diamond made it his personal crusade that the Vikings would not be late for their game in Detroit the following year.

So Diamond went to work and found an alternate route from the team's hotel to the Silverdome. The route avoided the freeway and used suburban streets. Still, Diamond asked Grant if the team could leave 15 minutes earlier just in case. Remembering the embarrassing disaster of the year before, Grant agreed to change his schedule just that once.

Of course, the Vikings' buses breezed right to the stadium. "We got there in 10 minutes and Bud wasn't happy then because we were so early," Diamond said.

When Diamond got off the bus, he encountered Grant. The stoic coach didn't say a word, but just looked at his watch and shot Diamond a disapproving look.

"It was that famous Bud Grant look," Diamond said. "One year we were too late, and the next we were too early."

YOU WANT THE COACHES TO DO WHAT?

The Vikings and the Cardinals played in the first NFL game in London, England in 1983. It was one of the first games played overseas, and the logistics were difficult to pull off.

However, the biggest difference for the Vikings was translating through the cultural differences.

During meeting days before the game the differences became downright comical. It almost became an episode of Three's Company. You know, a major misunderstanding.

Jeff Diamond was representing the Vikings in the meeting with the English game officials at the famed Wembley Stadium. One of the final logistics Diamond was trying to put together was figuring out where the Vikings' coaches were going to sit in the press box for the game.

The English officials were dumbfounded when Diamond asked about the coaches. Coaches? Why in the world would the team need their coaches in the press box?

To comminute with the players, Diamond insisted. How? the English folks asked. By headsets, Diamond countered.

Put headsets on the coaches? the English officials wondered. Yes, said Diamond.

How would we even get the coaches up to the press box? the English asked, growing more incredulous by the moment. By elevator, Diamond said as he was becoming more confused himself.

The coaches were too big for the elevators, the English said.

Finally, Diamond asked for clarification.

Coaches in England, of course, are buses.

"Could you imagine," Diamond said. "They thought I wanted the players to talk to our buses through headsets."

THAT HURTS

Losing to the Vikings is always painful for the Green Bay Packers and their faithful.

But a last-moment defeat at the Metrodome on Nov. 5, 1995, was particularly agonizing for Green Bay coach Mike Holmgren.

In an infamous day—known in Wisconsin at "the T. J. Rubley Game"—Rubley, the third-string quarterback, was leading the team toward the end zone late in the game with the score tied at 24-24. With the Packers nearing field-goal range, Rubley ignored a call by Holmgren and audibled on a play. It was a poor decision.

Rubley was intercepted and the Vikings drive in for the game-winning field goal.

Still infuriated, Holmgren punched a light fixture in the Metrodome hallway on the way to the visiting locker room. The punch fractured Holmgren's hand, doubling his pain. Rubley was not back with the team the next year.

SEE YOU WEDNESDAY

There is a three-word phrase that means the world to the NFL player during a tiring season.

It's not "I love you," but it's just as heartwarming.

"See you Wednesday."

NFL players hear those words and they go nuts. It's as if they had just won the lottery. "See you Wednesday" means the coach has just given the team Monday off to go along with the usual Tuesday off day every team gets and doesn't want to see them until Wednesday to prepare for the next game. Basically, "See you Wednesday" means the players just got an impromptu weekend off.

Mondays in the NFL are days dedicated to review of the previous day's film work and weightlifting along with some light preparation for the next Sunday's opponent.

"See You Wednesday" is only given after a huge win as a reward. The coach usually springs it on the players at the end of his postgame speech.

"It's a reward they all want," coach Dennis Green said. "It means something special to them."

FAR OUT, MAN

In 1990, the Vikings became the most progressive team in all of sports. Or at least the most creative. General manager Mike Lynn thought something drastic, even radical, had to be done to create team chemistry.

The two previous seasons, the Vikings were as talented as any team in the NFL, but they couldn't put it all together. The team didn't always get along well and didn't play together as they should.

Desperate, Lynn came up with the unique idea of taking the team to a seminar promoting New Age togetherness in Santa Fe, New Mexico, in May. So instead of staying in the Twin Cities for another mundane May minicamp, the team flew down and spent the weekend on the Pecos River.

The team took lessons in trust and togetherness. Among the exercises they participated in were walking tightropes, bungee jumping and leading each other blindfolded.

"It was supposed to make us a family," Jeff Diamond said. "It was different, to say the least."

The players enjoyed the unorthodox weekend, but things didn't always go as hoped.

Diamond had to maneuver a blindfolded Bucky Scribner through a desert. Diamond led the trusting punter right into a cactus. Scribner squealed in agony.

"I felt terrible," Diamond said. "The poor guy was trusting me and I had him walk right into a cactus."

So, did the unique experience pay dividends?

"Probably not," Diamond said in retrospect. "The two previous years we were good. That year we went 6-10 with the same personnel. We may have liked each other better and been closer, but we weren't any good."

OLD FRIENDS REUNITE

Nearly 20 years have passed, and Joe Kapp and Paul Wiggin have various versions and memories of perhaps the craziest play in college football history.

As does every meeting between the old friends, the conversation often turns to "The Play."

"He said, "'You sacked me in college, you got me,'" Wiggin said. "I looked at him and said, 'But you got the last laugh, you [jerk].' We can laugh about it."

Kapp, a Vikings quarterback from 1967-69 and in their first Super Bowl appearance, and Wiggin, the Vikings' director of pro scouting who has been with the team since 1985, spoke recently on the bizarre event of Nov. 20, 1982. Both former coaches have been flooded by media requests regarding the 20th anniversary of what some sports historians say was the most unusual play in sports.

The game between two of college football's biggest rivals, Stanford, coached by Wiggin, and California, coached by Kapp, ended when Cal used five laterals to score on a 57-yard kickoff return on the final play. The play ended when Cal's Kevin Moen crashed into Gary Tyrrell, a trombone player for Stanford's renegade marching band, in the end zone, giving the Golden Bears an improbable 25-20 victory.

The band, along with several hundred Stanford fans, charged onto Cal's Memorial Stadium field with four seconds left to celebrate a Peach Bowl berth. Instead, Cal came away with a disputed touchdown and a victory in the final collegiate game for Stanford quarterback John Elway. Ever since, it has been known simply as "The Play."

MEMORIES OF THE PLAY

"Miserable, agonizing" is the way Wiggin remembers it. "Brilliant coaching" is Kapp's tongue-in-cheek recollection. Each coach has replayed the football version of a fire drill in his mind many times since that chilly day in Berkeley. Neither has changed his mind about it. Wiggin still believes the play was illegal. Kapp still disagrees.

Wiggin said he long ago accepted that he would be forever connected to The Play. Whether he sees replays of it every college season or whether Kapp stops by to remind him, The Play lives on.

"I realized it early," Wiggin said. "To get away, in the days after The Play, I went to Virginia for Thanksgiving. I hadn't even checked into the hotel yet and a guy in line said, 'Hey, aren't you that coach from The Play?'"

SWITCHING UP

To help the Vikings loosen up after they lost their first three games of the 2002 season, Tice had his players step into each other's shoes. Or at least their jerseys.

The team practiced at the Seahawks' stadium on the day before the game and Tice had players spontaneously switch jerseys with another player. Daunte Culpepper and right tackle Chris Liwienski switched jerseys and so did massive center Matt Birk and diminutive running back Michael Bennett.

"It's a little tight," Birk said of wearing the uniform of his much smaller teammate. "But it looks good."

Tice borrowed the idea from Chuck Knox, his coach in Seattle. Whenever the Seahawks practiced in another team's stadium, he'd do the switcheroo.

Chris Liwienski: The massive offensive lineman made the difficult transition from practice squad player to starter. (Photo courtesy of Andy Lyons/Getty Images)

WHO ARE YOU?

Long snapper Brody Liddiard, a tight end in name only, was sent onto the field on the Vikings' final drive when the team used a three-tight end set late in a game against Miami on Dec. 21, 2002. Byron Chamberlain was out with a sprained right ankle so Liddiard had to be paired with legitimate tight ends Jim Kleinsasser and Hunter Goodwin.

Liddiard had never played on offense for the team, so his presence shocked his teammates. When he saw Liddiard in the huddle, Culpepper tried to shoo him a way.

"I threw him out of the huddle," Culpepper said of seeing Liddiard on a crucial fourth and two from the Dolphins' 45 with 2:07 remaining and the game tied at 17-17.

Liddiard was surprised to be there himself. Moss had to help him get aligned on the line.

"I was just out there," Liddiard said. "My mind was just spinning. I was just blocking and hoping everything would turn out OK."

THE WIND CAN'T DO THAT

In the days after Gary Anderson's improbable 53-yard field goal to beat Miami in 2001, whispers came out of Miami insinuating that the Vikings may have manipulated the elements. Yes, some folks in Miami thought the Vikings quickly whipped up some wind to assist Anderson in his longest field goal in years.

When the doors of the hallway connecting the street and the pavilion of the Metrodome are open at the same time, it creates a wind affect that is fairly potent. Well, as legend in Miami has it, the Vikings opened all the hallway doors in the Metrodome, creating a wind to assist Anderson's leg.

"Hogwash" said the Vikings, and "impossible" said the experts.

"That's crazy," Tice said with a laugh. "I wish I would have thought of that one."

Bill Lester, who helps run the Metrodome, said whispers of such phantom wind storms have been urban legend dating back to the Twins' 1987 World Series championship against St. Louis. Lester said a physicist was brought in to do a study inside the Metrodome, and he said it was impossible to create wind that would affect a football or baseball's path.

"Sounds like sour grapes to me," said Lester. "It can't be done ... Gary Anderson did it all by himself."

THE FEUD

Before Rusty Tillman was the Vikings' special teams coach, he was an adversary of former Governor Jesse Ventura. Maybe it was best for everyone concerned that Ventura's four-year term as governor had expired two weeks prior to Tillman being the newest Minnesota resident.

The Ventura-Tillman spat was one of the most memorable moments of the one-year XFL that was run by the World Wrestling Federation. In February 2001, Ventura, a color television commentator for the league, called New York/New Jersey Hitmen head coach Tillman "gutless" for having a player kick a field goal rather than going for a touchdown. Tillman shot back in a sidelines interview a few minutes later, saying Ventura "wouldn't know if a football was pumped or stuffed."

As the game ended, Minnesota's governor went onto the field to interview Tillman, whose team won the game 13-0. Tillman stormed off, though. "Ain't you gonna talk to me?" the governor asked.

"I got nothing to say to Jesse Ventura," Tillman told another announcer as he jogged off. Ventura then addressed the national television audience by saying: "I got him intimidated, there's no doubt about it. The guy couldn't wait to get off the field. He's afraid of me." In future weeks, Ventura was purposely assigned to cover Tillman's games and continued to try to goad the coach. Tillman never bit.

Two years later, Tillman said the feud was real to him even though he thinks the XFL and perhaps even NBC, which broadcast the games, tried to stage the spat.

"I told [XFL commissioner] Vince McMahon going in that I'm volatile and I didn't want to participate in that type of stuff, I just wanted to coach football," Tillman said. "They hired Jesse and they wanted to get someone to make me go off. But I wouldn't do it as much as he tried. It was like a bully in school. They keep bugging you until you ignore them and then they go away. It was like that with him."

BALL BOYS

Perhaps no NFL team can boast an alumni group of training camp ball boys as the Vikings can. The Vikings' lineage of camp helpers is stunningly impressive.

Among those who served as ball boys for the Vikings are Indianapolis Colts quarterback Peyton Manning, his brother, Mississippi quarterback Eli Manning, former Vikings receiver Troy Walters, and Pittsburgh All-America receiver Larry Fitzgerald, Jr.

The Manning boys were at camp when their father Archie was a Vikings quarterback in 1983-84. Walters was at camp as a teen before becoming an All-American at Stanford. His father, Trent, was a Vikings assistant. Troy Walters came full circle in 2000 when he was drafted to play receiver for the Vikings.

"I know this camp well," Walters said. "It's strange to be back as a player."

Fitzgerald was a ball boy as a Minneapolis high schooler. His father was a friend of the program, enabling Fitzgerald's presence at camp.

Fitzgerald became an instant Heisman Trophy candidate and credited his time in camp with Randy Moss and Cris Carter as a head start. Both pros helped Fitzgerald refine his game. Carter continued his relationship, attending Fitzgerald's game at Miami as a freshman. Fitzgerald didn't let down his mentor. He caught three touchdowns as Pittsburgh nearly upset the No. 1 ranked Miami Hurricanes.

FIGHTING SPIRIT

If you took a poll of Vikings players over the years regarding the player most likely to continue playing after the whistle, tight end Hunter Goodwin would likely be the overwhelming winner.

The stout, rowdy Texan loves a good tussle, and he isn't afraid to show it. If the tight end were a hockey player, he certainly would be a goon.

"Just a tough guy," coach Mike Tice said. "Hunter is not afraid of anyone."

There usually isn't a game that goes by without Goodwin getting in some type of shoving match. He was fined three times in the 2002 season alone for his extracurricular activities.

Perhaps the moment that best categorized Goodwin came in 2002 when the blocking specialist caught his first touchdown of the season against Atlanta. Instead of spiking the football like most players do, Goodwin found the nearest Falcons defender and pushed him.

"I just wasn't used to scoring," Goodwin said with a laugh. "I did what comes naturally."

TOENAILS?

Sometimes tempers flare in football. And sometimes even teammates fight.

And we're not just talking about on the practice field. Sometimes the fracas carries over to the locker room.

In the mid 1990s, the Vikings' locker room was the site for one of the most exciting bouts in team history.

And it was all over toenails. That's right, toenails.

Tight end Adrian Cooper was clipping his toenails and creating quite a mess, according to eyewitnesses. Veteran defensive tackle Henry Thomas complained to the much younger player that he shouldn't be spreading his disposed nails in the locker room.

Cooper disrespected Thomas and, suddenly, it was let's-get-ready-to-rumble time.

The two went at it feverishly. Then, suddenly, defensive tackle John Randle, coming to Thomas's rescue—defense has to stand up for defense, of course—rushed Cooper and a full-on brawl ensued.

"You don't want to see that type of stuff between team-mates, but boys will be boys," one Vikings defensive player who witnessed the fight said. "Boy, that was a memorable one."

GREAT FINISH

The 2002 Vikings were an interesting team to follow. Although they lost 10 games, the Vikings finished the season as one of the hottest teams in the NFL. They won their final three games of the season, making them only the fourth team with a losing record in the past 10 seasons to win their final three games.

However, there was nothing easy about the Vikings' strong finish. Their last three games were all decided in the final moments.

Against New Orleans on Dec. 15, the Vikings bucked NFL sanity and went for two points instead of settling for an extra point that would have sent the game to overtime. However, Mike Tice's gutsy call prevailed and so did the Vikings, 32-31. The next week, Gary Anderson's mammoth 53-yard field goal with 17 seconds remaining iced the Dolphins at the Metrodome. In the season finale at Detroit, the Vikings survived a ferocious Lions rally. Detroit missed a two-point conversion that would have sent the game to overtime, giving the Vikings the victory.

"We should have expected this," a relieved Greg Biekert said after the final game. "We don't blow out anyone. But we are survivors."

Epilogue

Nine National Football League seasons have passed since *Tales From the Vikings Locker Room* was first published. Six different teams have been crowned Super Bowl champion since 2003. Unfortunately for the Vikings, none of those six champions wore the Minnesota purple and gold. (Even worse, Green Bay *is* one of those six champions.)

While the pinnacle of professional football has continued to elude Minnesota since this book was first released, few franchises have made more headlines in the past nine years than the Vikings.

THE COLLAPSE

The big headline from 2003: the Vikings became the first team in NFL history to start the season 6-0 and miss the playoffs. Minnesota cruised to a great start behind the very familiar Daunte Culpepper/Randy Moss combo. Moss would end up leading the league in touchdowns and finishing second in both receptions and receiving yards during the '03 season. But a below-average defense and a rash of untimely turnovers forced the Vikings into a must-win situation heading into Week 17.

The Vikings faced the 3-12 Arizona Cardinals, a team with seven straight losses leading up to the contest. Most Vikings fans won't like reliving this painful memory, but the season ended abruptly when Josh McCown found Nate Poole in the end zone to clinch a double-digit, fourth-quarter comeback for the Cardinals. Even for a fan base that had sadly grown accustomed to horrible letdowns, this stomach punch of a loss stood out. If the 2003 Vikings' epic collapse had happened today, fans would have to endure the McCown-to-Poole replay roughly 2.3 million times more than they did then, thanks to Facebook, Twitter, and the 24-hour sports news cycle. Let's just move on.

MOON OVER LAMBEAU

The 2004 season was a lot like the previous campaign: a solid start through six games (5-1) followed by a collapse down the stretch (the Vikings lost four of their last five to finish 8-8). More high-flying offense led by Culpepper and Moss. More porous defense. More inconsistency leading to a roller coaster of results. But this time around, the Vikings managed to back into the playoffs to face the Packers at Lambeau Field. Green Bay had won nine of their last eleven games to clinch the NFC North; Brett Favre and the Packers were heavily favored. But Culpepper threw for four touchdowns while Favre threw four interceptions and the Vikings cruised to a 31-17 victory.

Any Vikings fan will tell you that beating the Packers is wonderful no matter when it happens. Randy Moss helped add a little flair to the victory by faux-mooning the Lambeau crowd after his fourth quarter touchdown iced the contest. It would end up being Moss' final victory in a Vikings jersey for six years (more on that later), but the image of the lanky wide receiver pretending to drop his drawers remains an iconic one in Vikings folklore.

As for the team's playoff run, it ended with a 27-14 loss to the Eagles, in a game marred by Vikings turnovers, penalties, and missed opportunities.

CHANGES

The 2005 season was bookended by great change in Minnesota—not in the results (another up-and-down 9-7 record, narrowly missing the playoffs) but in the personnel. Moss's antics had worn thin on the Vikings front office. In the last game of the regular season, on January 2nd , he headed to the locker room before the end of a loss to the Redskins. Off the field, he was arrested for bumping into a Minneapolis traffic cop with his vehicle, and he dropped the infamous "Straight Cash Homey" quote after being fined for the Lambeau Moon. The Vikings traded Moss to the Oakland Raiders before the 2005 season in return for the #7 overall pick and linebacker Napoleon Harris.

The trade turned out to be mutually destructive. The Vikings drafted Troy Williamson with the draft pick from Oakland, who is widely regarded as the biggest draft bust in team history. Meanwhile, Moss never really got his career back on track until he moved from the Raiders to the Patriots in 2007.

Moss' longtime battery mate, Daunte Culpepper, also saw his Vikings career come to an abrupt end in 2005. Culpepper struggled to a 2-4 start that included throwing only six touchdowns against twelve interceptions without his go-to receiver. It went from bad to worse for Culpepper as he shattered his knee in a Week 8 loss to the Carolina Panthers. The Vikings shipped their former franchise quarterback to Miami after the season was over.

Even though the Vikings rallied to win seven of their last nine games of the 2005 season under veteran backup Brad

Johnson, it wasn't enough for Head Coach Mike Tice to keep his job. Another change that happened in 2005 was in the Vikings' ownership—Red McCombs sold the team to a group led by Zygi Wilf in May 2005. Although most Vikings players liked Tice and the team finished above .500, Tice wasn't Wilf's "guy." So he was jettisoned in favor of former Eagles offensive coordinator Brad Childress.

LET THE CHILDRESS ERA BEGIN

The seventh Minnesota Vikings Head Coach started his career a lot like Tice had in 2003 and 2004. Childress's team charged out to a 4-2 start behind the arm of the 38-year-old Johnson and the legs of newly acquired running back Chester Taylor. Taylor thrived after being in Jamal Lewis' shadow for four years in Baltimore, racking up over 1,500 yards from scrimmage in 2006.

But like the other Vikings teams that got off to promising starts earlier in the decade, the 2006 squad faltered badly down the stretch. Rookie QB Tarvaris Jackson started the last two games of a 6-10 season that went out with a whimper. In retrospect, 2006 was always a rebuilding year. When Travis Taylor is your leading receiver and Darrion Scott leads the team with a whopping 5.5 sacks, it's not like hopes were bursting through the Metrodome roof to begin with. If you don't remember much about the 2006 season, don't worry about it—nobody does.

THE ARRIVAL OF A SAVIOR

The Vikings' poor finish in 2006 assured them of the seventh overall pick in the 2007 draft. While the franchise completely whiffed on Williamson with the same pick two years earlier, Minnesota struck gold by landing prized running back Adrian Peterson this time around. A.D. (for "All Day") or A.P. (whichever acronym you prefer) hit the ground running—literally. And his running made others hit the ground—literally. The bruising rookie with otherworldly athleticism amassed over 1,600 yards from scrimmage and 13 touchdowns in his NFL debut. Peterson made countless "wow" plays in his first year out of Oklahoma, but one accomplishment stood out above everything else.

On November 4, 2007, the Vikings welcomed the San Diego Chargers to the Metrodome. The Chargers had just demolished three straight opponents and were allowing only 89 yards per game on the ground. The 2-5 Vikings were down by a touchdown at halftime while A.P. had a pedestrian 43 yards rushing. The only thing that seemed special about the game was that Antonio Cromartie had scored the longest touchdown in NFL history off a missed Ryan Longwell field goal as time expired in the second quarter.

But the last 30 minutes were definitely worth sticking around for.

Peterson went absolutely bonkers in the second half, constantly gashing the Chargers for long runs and making would-be tacklers look like traffic cones. A.P. ended up with an NFL-record 296 yards rushing, a single-game record that still stands. Unfortunately Peterson's all-world performance was the only major highlight of the 2007 season as the Vikings sputtered to an 8-8 finish and missed the playoffs for the third consecutive year. At least the prodigious running back's arrival gave Vikings fans something that they hadn't experienced in a while: hope.

BACK TO THE PLAYOFFS

One year after bolstering their offense with an impact player, the Vikings improved their defense by adding a big name in 2008. Minnesota acquired All-Pro Kansas City defensive end Jared Allen in exchange for a first- and two third-round draft picks. The draft picks and huge contract (the Vikings gave Allen a six year, $72 million deal) were considered a risk with Allen's off-field problems in Kansas City, but Allen proved to clean up both on and off the field.

Allen joined the Williams Wall–defensive tackles Kevin and Pat Williams–to create one of the most formidable defensive lines in the league. The mulleted manhandler recorded 14.5 sacks and earned First-team All-Pro and Pro Bowl honors during his first season in purple.

However, the team still sputtered to an 0-2 start due to shaky quarterback play by Jackson. Childress quickly pulled the incumbent starter in favor of veteran journeyman Gus Frerotte. While Frerotte rarely made it look pretty, the Vikings started winning. They went 8-3 under Frerotte until he was hurt in a Week 14 win against Detroit. Once again, here came Jackson.

Poor Tarvaris. Throughout his tenure in Minnesota, Jackson had his playing time and starting status yanked around more frequently than Lucy pulling the football away from Charlie Brown. Although Jackson had a career day in his first start back and helped the Vikings clinch the NFC North title on the final week of the season, his success would be short-lived. He (and just about every other player wearing purple that day) played horribly as the Vikings were drummed out of the Metrodome and playoffs by the Philadelphia Eagles.

Well, at least the Vikings had finally made the playoffs again! And after signing Sage Rosenfels in the following offseason, the battle for starting quarterback would be the main storyline of the 2009 Vikings. Right?

Well...not so much.

FAVREGEDDON

It was the patriarch of the Hatfields joining forces with the McCoys. It was the CEO of Coca-Cola professing his love for Pepsi. It was oil suddenly deciding that mixing with water was just fine. But here it was.

By the summer of 2009, the Brett Favre Media Circus had become an annual tradition. After years of will-he-or-won't-he-retire talk with the Packers, Favre finally called it quits only to join the New York Jets in 2008. But after tearing his biceps tendon mid-way through the season, the Ol' Gunslinger ultimately fell short in the Big Apple, going 9-7 and missing the playoffs.

So he retired. Again. Yet as training camp started for the Vikings, rumors were swirling that Favre wanted to join his longtime adversaries in Minnesota. The reasons made sense: Favre alledgedly wanted to stick it to Packers GM Ted Thompson, and the Vikings were a quarterback away from being a legitimate contender. But surely, there was no way that Vikings fans would find themselves rooting for someone they spent so many years loathing, right?

Think again.

On August 17, Favre signed a contract with the Vikings, replete with helicopter coverage of Childress picking him up at the airport and over-covered press conferences. Some Packers fans immediately swore off their idol for his treason. Others immediately swore allegiance to the Vikings, following their hero across the border. Any way you sliced it, everyone knew they were suddenly in for a very entertaining Minnesota Vikings season.

And did Favre ever deliver. Favre's home debut as a Viking? A 32-yard pass to the back of the end zone as time expired for an impossible comeback victory over San Francisco. Favre's debut against his old team, a Green Bay squad that Childress had defeated exactly once leading up to that game? Another

W. The return trip to Lambeau, his first time playing there as an opponent? No problem. Even after a few prime time clunkers down the stretch, the Vikings finished the season as the NFC North champions and earned a first-round bye in the NFC playoffs.

The Vikings welcomed the Cowboys to town for the Divisional round and it wasn't even a contest. Favre tossed four touchdowns and the defense forced three turnovers in a 34-3 rout. Next up: the NFC Championship in New Orleans.

Every Vikings fan remembers how heartbreaking the 1998 NFC Championship was; this one might have been worse.

The Vikings absolutely dominated the game but couldn't seem to get out of their own way. They ended up outgaining the Saints by over 200 yards, but they fumbled six—SIX—times, losing three. Favre was absolutely pounded by the Saints defense throughout the game; some of them seemed like blatant cheap shots well after the ball was out of Favre's hands. (Thanks to the Saints' bounty scandal that was announced by the league in 2012, we now know that many of those hits may have had financial motivation behind them.)

Yet somehow, amid all the turnovers and dirty plays, the Vikings managed to tie the game with five minutes remaining. As time wound down, it was time for one more magical chapter in Brett Favre's legacy.

Or so we thought. Favre marched the Vikings down into Longwell's field goal range with under a minute remaining. But an inexplicable 12 men on the field penalty moved them back out of range. On third down, Favre rolled right and had roughly six acres of space to run. Maybe it was the beating he took; maybe it was his unshakable Gunslinger mentality taking over. Either way, Favre elected to throw across his body toward his favorite target, Sidney Rice.

You know the rest. Interception. Overtime. The Vikings don't see the ball again. Two weeks later, the Saints are celebrating their first Super Bowl victory. Not the Vikings.

In the end, Favre made the kind of mistake that used to make Vikings fans giggle with schadenfreude. He brought his team to the precipice of glory only to literally throw it away at the last second.

Although the loss stung, fans were optimistic that the Vikings had the nucleus returning to make another run at a championship.

Boy, were they wrong.

IT ALL FALLS DOWN

The 2010 season for the Minnesota Vikings might as well be remembered as "The Murphy's Law Year". Everything that could have gone wrong did, and in spectacular fashion.

With the season going south in a hurry and Childress losing control of his team, the Vikings called on an old friend before their Week 5 Monday night matchup with the Jets— the one and only Randy Moss. Vikings fans were ecstatic to have their prodigal son back, but it became abundantly clear that this iteration of Randy wasn't like the version everyone remembered. After just four games and a tirade or two against everything from Childress' game planning to catering, #84 was gone just as quickly as he had arrived.

The Moss debacle put additional strain on the already shaky relationship between Childress and Zygi Wilf. In fact, Wilf nearly parted ways with Childress instead of releasing Moss. Childress was finally fired just three weeks later after an especially embarrassing home loss to the Packers in Week 11. Even though his team was crumbling around him, Childress insisted that his "Kick Ass Offense" system would work if the players would only buy into it. He was constantly spotted either bickering with or being completely ignored by Favre on the sidelines before getting canned.

While Childress didn't seem to have it anymore, Favre clearly didn't either. His ironman starting streak of 297 games finally ended after a crushing blow in Week 13 against Buffalo.

And just to make sure everyone knew that this wasn't the Vikings' year, the roof literally caved in. A nasty December snowstorm caused the Metrodome roof to collapse, forcing the Vikings to play their last two "home" games in Detroit and at the University of Minnesota.

The magical run of 2009 seemed like decades ago. Once again, the Vikings were rebuilding.

PONDERING THE FUTURE

With Favre retired for good this time—no really, he didn't come back (yet)—it was time for the Vikings to look in another direction at quarterback. Minnesota turned some heads by drafting Christian Ponder of Florida State University with the 12th overall pick in the 2011 draft. Since they didn't want to throw the unpolished rookie to the wolves right away, they picked up another very experienced quarterback in Donovan McNabb. After McNabb's poor showing in Washington the year before, critics were skeptical that he had anything left in the tank. On the other hand, McNabb could be the perfect transition to the quarterback of the future if he could regain his old form.

He didn't regain his old form.

McNabb's favorite passing target seemed to be the ground. After a dismal 1-5 start Ponder was thrust into the starting role. Unfortunately the change in quarterback didn't bring a change of results: Ponder spent most of his time scrambling for his life behind a porous offensive line and throwing to mediocre receivers (outside of the electric Percy Harvin, of course).

The losses—13 in all, tied for the most in franchise history—weren't just on the scoreboard either. Adrian Peterson went down with a torn ACL in the second to last game of the year. Jim Kleinsasser, the punishing H-back who spent his entire career with the Vikings, retired after the season.

THE MINNESOTA (NOT LOS ANGELES) VIKINGS

If the 2011 season wasn't bad enough, the Vikings faced one of their toughest opponents of all time immediately afterward: Minnesota state legislation. Even with the new roof, the Metrodome is a relic amongst other NFL stadia. With the team's stadium lease expiring and Los Angeles hungry for an NFL franchise, the Vikings faced the very real possibility of following the Lakers and North Stars out of Minnesota.

Things looked bleak at first. For months, state legislators couldn't even agree where to put a theoretical stadium much less pass a bill for it. After countless hours of debate, endless theories of how to fund the stadium, and roadblocks at every turn, a bill was finally drafted. The new stadium would be right where the current, old stadium presides in Minneapolis.

The voting was close—really, really close—but thanks to the unwavering support of Vikings diehards, the bill passed in May 2012.

There is still a lot of work for the Vikings to do if they ever want to win that elusive Super Bowl, but at least we know that they'll be chasing it in their home state (and new home stadium in 2016) for years and years to come.